The Heinemann Science Scheme

Book 2

Ian Bradley • Peter Gale • Mark Winterbottom

This book is dedicated to the following people:

From Ian Bradley: To Jean and Denis Bradley – now will you listen to my energy advice?

From Peter Gale: To Alan Quarterman and Ena Tatler, great teachers and good friends.

From Mark Winterbottom: To Sal, for continuing to put up with never seeing me!

Heinemann Educational Publishers
Halley Court, Jordan Hill, Oxford, OX2 8EJ
a division of Reed Educational & Professional Publishing Ltd
Heinemann is a registered trademark of Reed Educational &
Professional Publishing Ltd

OXFORD MELBOURNE AUCKLAND
JOHANNESBURG BLANTYRE GABORONE
IBADAN PORTSMOUTH NH (USA) CHICAGO

© Ian Bradley, Peter Gale, Mark Winterbottom, 2001

First published 2001

ISBN 0 435 58244 5

05 04 03 02 01
10 9 8 7 6 5 4 3

Edited by Liz Jones and Mary Korndorffer

Designed and typeset by Cambridge Publishing Management Ltd

Illustrated by Hardlines

Original illustrations © Heinemann Educational Publishers, 2001

Printed and bound in the Uk by Bath Colourbooks

Index by Paul Nash

Acknowledgements
The authors and publishers would like to thank the following for
permission to use photographs:
Cover photo by Science Photo Library

Page 135, illustration of red ball adapted from 'Make Colour Work
for You', Readers Digest, published by The Readers Digest
Association Limted, from the series 'The Kodak Guide to Creative
Photography, 1983, copyright Kodak Limited. This volume
copyright 1983 Kodak Limited, Mitchell Beazley Publishers, Salvat
Editores, S.A.

p2 Peter Gould, p3 T and M Peter Gould, p4 T: Peter Gould, B:
SPL/Biophotos, p5 Peter Gould, p7 Corbis, p8 John Frost, p11, 13
Peter Gould, p14 T: SPL/Alfred Pasieka, B: Peter Gould, p16
SPL/Cordelia Molloy, p17 Peter Gould, p19 T: SPL/Biophotos, B:
SPL Manfred Cage, p20 SPL/Eric Grave, p23 T: Corbis, B:
Corbis/Galen Rowell, p26 Peter Gould, p27 Ginny Stroud Lewis, p28
T: SPL/Dr Jeremy Burgess, M and B: Peter Gould, p29 T: SPL/tek
Image, B: SPL, p30, 31 Peter Gould, p32 SPL/Matt Meadows/ Peter
Arnold Inc, p34 Collections, p35 Corbis, p36 SPL, p37
SPL/Biophotos, p38, 39 Peter Gould, p40 SPL, p42 SPL/Saturn Stills,
p44 GSF, p45 GSF, p46 GSF, p47 T: GSF, T/M Corbis/Papillo, B/M
GSF, B: GSF, p48 Andrew Lambert, p50 T: Heather Angel, B: Ginny
Stroud Lewis, p55, 56 Peter Gould, p57 T: Peter Morris, B: SPL, p58
SPL, p60, 62 Peter Gould, p63 Peter Morris, p68 T: Peter Gould, T/M
and B/M: Corbis, B: SPL, p 71, 74 Peter Gould, p75 T: Peter Gould, B:
SPL, p76 T: SPL, T/M: Corbis, B/M: SPL, B:SPL, p77 GSF, p78 T:
Ginny Stroud Lewis, M: GSF, B: SPL, p79 T: GSF, B: SPL, p80 Corbis,
p82, SPL, p83, 84, 86 Corbis, p87 T: SPL, B: Corbis, p88 T: Corbis, B:
GSF, p89 T/L: GSF, T/M: Corbis, T/R: GSF, B/L: GSF, B/M: GSF, B/R:
SPL, p90 T: GSF, M: Peter Gould, B: SPL, p91 GSF, p93 GSF, Corbis
and SPL, p94, 95 GSF, p96 Andrew Lambert, p101, 102, 106 Peter
Gould, p107 L: Corbis, R: Peter Gould, p108 Andrew Lambert/Peter
Gould, p109 T: SPL, B: Peter Gould, p110, p111 Peter Gould, p112
SPL/ Peter Morris, p114, 116-118, 121-123, 125 Peter Gould, p131
Corbis, p132 Peter Gould, p136 T, T/M and B/M: Corbis, B: Peter
Gould, p137 T: Peter Morris, B: Corbis, p138 Peter Gould, p142
Corbis, p144 Peter Morris.

SPL = Science Photo Library
GSF = Geoscience Photo Library
T = Top, M = Middle, B = Bottom, L = Left, R = Right

The publishers have made every effort to trace the copyright
holders, but if they have inadvertently overlooked any, they will be
pleased to make the necessary arrangements at the first opportunity.

Picture research by Ginny Stroud Lewis

Welcome to Heinemann Science Scheme!

This is the second book in a series of three which covers all the science you need to learn at Key Stage 3.

It is divided into twelve units. Each unit has topics which take up a double page spread. On each double page spread you will find:

● **A topic checklist at the start with this heading:**

> TOPIC CHECKLIST

This tells you what you will study on that double page spread.

● **Questions as you go along like this:**

> **ⓑ** **What is the solute in salt solution?**

These are quick questions which help you check that you understand the explanations before you carry on.

● **Questions in a box at the end of the spread with this heading:**

> QUESTIONS

These help you draw together all the material on the spread.

Important words are highlighted in bold on the pages. They all appear in a glossary at the back of the book with their meanings so that you can look them up easily as you work through the book.

As you study Heinemann Science Scheme you will also be doing practical activities and extra questions and assignments from the teacher's pack which goes with it, as well as tests which help you and your teachers keep track of how you're doing.

We hope you enjoy studying science with Heinemann Science Scheme.

Contents

A Food and digestion

WHAT IS IN FOOD?

TOPIC CHECKLIST

- What are the nutrients in food?
- Which foods give you which nutrients?
- How do you get water?

Different food groups

What are the nutrients in food?

Look at the foods in the picture. Each food helps your body to work properly. Some foods help you **grow** and some foods give you **energy**. Because different foods have different jobs, you must eat lots of different foods to stay healthy.

a **Name one food from the picture which helps you to grow.**

b **Name one food from the picture which gives you energy.**

Food contains water, which is essential for survival. Food also contains **nutrients**. A nutrient is something in your food that is needed by and used by the body. There are six different types of nutrient in food:

fat	carbohydrate	protein
vitamins	minerals	fibre

Nutrient	Which foods are good sources of this nutrient?
fats	butter, cooking oil, cream
carbohydrates, e.g. sugar and starch	rice, bread, potatoes
proteins	meat, fish, eggs
fibre (this is also called roughage)	fruit, vegetables, brown bread, cereal, brown rice
minerals, e.g. iron, calcium, sodium, iodine	meat, milk, salt, seafood
vitamins, e.g. A, B_1, B_2, C, D, E	fruit, vegetables, cereal

Which foods give you which nutrients?

Different foods contain different nutrients. Some foods are good sources of one nutrient and others are good sources of another nutrient.

Different foods contain different amounts of each nutrient. You can see how much they contain by looking at the **nutritional label** on the side of the packet.

If you look at the label of any food, most of it will be made of carbohydrates, fats, proteins, fibre and water. All foods contain very small amounts of vitamins and minerals, although some contain more than others. You only need very small amounts of vitamins and minerals.

c **Look at the labels in the photographs. Which food contains the largest amount of protein?**

d **Explain why is there less sodium than protein in food a.**

How do you get water?

About three quarters of your body is water, and you probably need to take in between two and three litres of water each day. That's like drinking 15 cups of water every day! Although you get most of your water from drinking, you also get some from food. Most foods contain small amounts of water.

a

NUTRITION INFORMATION

TYPICAL VALUES	Per 100g	Per Biscuit
Energy	2053kJ	70kJ
	490kcal	17kcal
Protein	10.4g	0.4g
Carbohydrate	55.5g	1.9g
(of which sugars)	3.5g	0.1g
Fat	25.2g	0.9g
(of which saturates)	15.3g	0.5g
Dietary Fibre	2.2g	0.1g
Sodium	1.0g	Trace

b

Nutrition Information		Per Bar	Per 100g
Energy	kJ	880	2260
	kcal	210	540
Protein	g	2.7	7.0
Carbohydrate	g	20.7	53.8
Fat	g	12.8	33.2

Ingredients: milk, sugar, cocoa butter, cocoa

e **Make a list of all the drinks you have had today. Every drink is made almost completely of water. How many cups of water have you drunk so far?**

f **Name three foods that contain a lot of water.**

Most foods contain water

QUESTIONS

1 What is a nutrient?

2 Write down the names of the six nutrients in food.

3 Write down one food that is a good source of:

   a fat   **b** fibre   **c** protein   **d** carbohydrate.

4 Give two ways in which your body gets water.

WHY IS FOOD IMPORTANT?

Why do you need nutrients?

Fats, proteins, carbohydrates and fibre all have very important jobs in your body. Look at the table to find out what they do. Remember though: fats and carbohydrates are not energy themselves, but are stores of energy. They are a bit like a battery. A battery is not electricity, but it is a store of electricity. Digesting food makes it possible for the energy to be released from fats and carbohydrates.

These are both energy stores

Nutrient	What's its job?
fat	an energy store a vital part of cell membranes
protein	for growth and repair of tissues
carbohydrate	an immediate source of energy
fibre	to keep waste moving through your digestive system fairly quickly

Vitamins and minerals occur in much smaller amounts in your diet. They all have different jobs inside your body. Look at the tables to find out why they are so important.

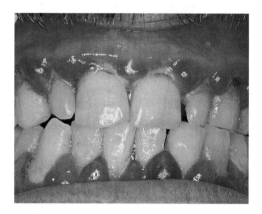

Without vitamin C your gums become unhealthy – a disease called scurvy

Vitamin	What's its job?
A	keeps skin healthy good eyesight in the dark
B	keeps nerves healthy
C	keeps gums healthy keeps skin healthy
D	keeps teeth and bones strong

Mineral	What's its job?
calcium and phosphorus	make teeth and bones strong
sodium	keeps nerves and muscles working properly
iron	helps the blood carry oxygen

ⓐ Name one mineral and one vitamin which are needed to keep your bones strong.

ⓑ Carrots contain vitamin A. Suggest what might happen to you if you do not eat any carrots.

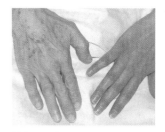

Without iron, you may look pale. Iron helps your blood to look red, and gives you rosy cheeks

Why do you need water?

Humans cannot survive without water! A person can live for up to 60 days without eating food, but will die within about three days without water. Water has some very important jobs inside your body.

Why do you need fibre?

You need fibre to make sure your digestive system works properly. Fibre absorbs water which makes it bulky. This gives the muscles in the walls of the digestive system something to push against so that they can keep food moving through the digestive system fairly quickly.

What does water do?	
Chemical reactions	Every chemical reaction in your body happens in water.
Excretion	Your body uses water to dissolve poisonous waste and to get rid of it in urine.
Transport	Water is used to move other nutrients around your body in the blood.
Cooling	Water cools the body down when you sweat.

What is a recommended daily allowance?

A **recommended daily allowance (RDA)** is the amount of a particular nutrient that you should eat each day to stay healthy. Breakfast cereals often show you how much of a nutrient's RDA you get in a bowl of cereal. Look at the information for thiamin in the label on the right.

The problem with RDA values is that they are not very accurate. They are the same for everyone. This can't be right, because everyone needs a slightly different balance of nutrients to survive. You'll find out why in the next topic.

NUTRITION INFORMATION			
	Typical value per 100g	30g serving with 125ml of semi-skimmed milk	
ENERGY	1550kJ	370kcal	700kJ*	170 kcal
PROTEIN	8g		7g
CARBOHYDRATES	82g		31g
of which sugars	8g		9g
starch	74g		22g
FAT	0.9g		2.5g*
of which saturates	0.2g		1.5g
FIBRE	3g		0.9g
SODIUM	1g		0.35g

THIAMIN (B1)	
1.2mg 85%RDA	0.4mg 30%RDA

Is necessary for the release of energy from carbohydrate.

Most breakfast cereals have a nutritional label

QUESTIONS

1 Why does your body need **a** fat, **b** carbohydrates, **c** protein and **d** fibre?

2 Choose two vitamins and explain their function in your body.

3 Choose two minerals and explain what happens to your body if it does not get enough of them.

4 Give three reasons why your body needs water.

A BALANCED DIET

> ## TOPIC CHECKLIST
>
> - What is a balanced diet?
> - Is a balanced diet the same for everyone?
> - Why do some people have special diets?

What is a balanced diet?

Your diet is what you eat. A balanced diet provides all the energy and nutrients that you need to stay healthy. It needs to be a balance of proteins, carbohydrates, fats, vitamins, minerals, fibre and water.

Nowadays, most people can eat a balanced diet if they choose to. But what do you think it was like when your parents or grandparents were children? In wartime, food was rationed in Britain. Do you think anyone ate a balanced diet then?

Food was scarce in wartime

Is a balanced diet the same for everyone?

A balanced diet is the diet that you need to stay healthy, but this may be different from the diet needed by somebody else. What affects the type of diet we need?

(a) **What do you think children ate for breakfast, at lunch-time, and for their evening meal during the Second World War?**

Size: The bigger you are, the more food you will need to survive.

Age: Young people tend to be very active. They need lots of carbohydrate and fat to give them energy. They are also growing quickly, and need lots of protein to make new body cells, lots of calcium and phosphorous to make teeth and bones, and lots of iron to make blood cells. Older people are less active and do not grow any more. They do not need to eat as much food.

Gender: Men and women need a slightly different balance of nutrients. Men tend to need more energy-rich nutrients (fat and carbohydrate) than women. Women need larger amounts of some vitamins and minerals, like vitamin B and iron.

Activity: If you are always playing sport, you will need to eat more carbohydrates and fats, which contain lots of energy. However, if you are someone like a weight-lifter, you will also need lots of protein to grow big muscles! Be careful though, if you are not very active and eat too much fat and carbohydrate, you will get fat!

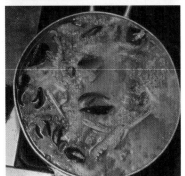

Culture: Our culture makes a big difference to what we eat. For example, in America and northern Europe, we tend to eat a lot of meat, while people from Italy and Spain eat a lot of fish. Some people, like Buddhists and some Hindus, do not eat meat at all, because it is against their beliefs. Look at the pictures; they show different types of food from lots of different cultures. All of them can form part of a healthy balanced diet.

Why do some people have special diets?

The balance of nutrients in some people's diet is very unusual. For example:

- People with heart disease must have a diet with very little fat.

- Pregnant women need extra protein, vitamins and minerals for their developing baby.

- A breast-feeding mother needs extra fat, proteins and carbohydrates to make milk for her baby.

Remember, such diets are still *balanced*; they are simply balanced to help these particular people stay healthy.

ⓑ **Vegetarians do not eat meat. What nutrients does meat contain?**

ⓒ **What other foods could vegetarians eat to obtain these nutrients?**

QUESTIONS

1 What is a balanced diet?

2 A balanced diet for one person is not necessarily a balanced diet for someone else. Explain why.

3 Suggest a balanced diet for an athlete
   a one week before a race, and
   b one day before a race.

4 Look at the graph. It shows how much protein, fat and carbohydrate are eaten by Gbemi. To eat the correct amount of each nutrient, she must have 100% of each nutrient's RDA. Which nutrient is lacking in her diet? Name one food she could eat to help balance her diet.

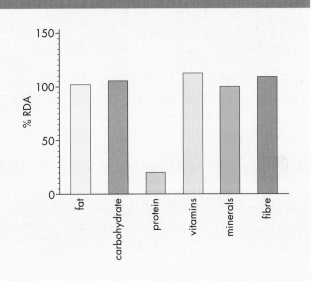

HOW DO YOU CHOOSE WHAT TO EAT?

TOPIC CHECKLIST

- Can we believe the adverts?
- What does the media say?
- What does research say?
- The best advice for a balanced diet

Can we believe the adverts?

You know that you should eat a balanced diet. But how do you know what to eat every day? In newspapers and magazines there are often adverts and articles about what we should eat, but think very carefully before taking their advice.

They may be written by the companies that make the food. To make you buy their food, they will try to convince you that it is healthy.

What does the media say?

Newspapers often report 'scare-stories' about food: they sell more papers that way. When you read an article about food, try to work out if you really are reading the facts.

Exclusive: Millions of cans in Benzene contamination alert

FIZZY DRINKS HEALTH SCARE

DOUBLE ALERT ON EGG AND CHICKENS PERIL

NOW FOOT AND MOUTH SPREADS TO HUMANS

APPLE JUICE IN CANCER SCARE

Some information may be unreliable . . .

What does research say?

You can also get information about diet based on scientific research. Some of this information comes from health promotion organisations like the British Heart Foundation. Some of the information comes from food marketing organisations like the Potato Marketing Board. When reading each organisation's advice, make sure you remember who wrote it.

- The British Heart Foundation will give you advice on what to eat for a healthy heart, but you also need to eat a diet to keep the rest of your body healthy.

- The Potato Marketing Board will tell you how good potatoes are for you. Just because they do not mention other vegetables, it does not mean you should not also eat them as part of a balanced diet.

The best advice for a balanced diet

If you can't find accurate advice, how do you decide what to eat? It is best to work on two basic principles:

1 You must not eat too much of any nutrient:

- If you have too much salt (which contains sodium), you can get high blood pressure, which can be harmful.

- If you eat too much fat or carbohydrate, your body will store the extra nutrients as fat under your skin, making you overweight.

2 You must not eat too little of any nutrient.

- If you have too little vitamin D, your bones and teeth will not stay strong and healthy.

- If you always eat low-calorie food, you will not get enough fat or carbohydrate, both of which are needed to keep you healthy.

. . . and some may be reliable

QUESTIONS

1 Jason says he has read that bananas are very good for you. He has decided to have only bananas for every meal. Explain to Jason why this may not be a good idea.

2 When Helga was young, she refused to drink milk because a newspaper said that it wasn't good for you. She is now an adult and is shorter than her friends who did drink milk. Explain why this might be.

WHAT HAPPENS TO FOOD INSIDE THE DIGESTIVE SYSTEM?

TOPIC CHECKLIST

- What does the digestive system do?
- What is digestion?
- What is absorption?

What does the digestive system do?

When you put food in your **mouth**, it goes through a long tube that runs from the mouth right through the body to the **anus**. Have a look at the diagram to see what the parts of this tube are called, and what each one does. The tube, and any other organs connected to it, are called the **digestive system**.

Food makes an amazing journey through the digestive system. During the journey, the food is broken down so that most of the nutrients are taken out of the food for the body to use. This process is called **digestion**. The nutrients are then small enough so that they can pass into your blood. This is called **absorption**.

What is digestion?

Most nutrients, including starch, protein and fat particles, are too big to get into the blood. Before they can be absorbed, they must be broken into smaller particles by digestion. It starts as soon as food enters the mouth and continues all the way through the digestive system. We will look more closely at the process of digestion in topic A6.

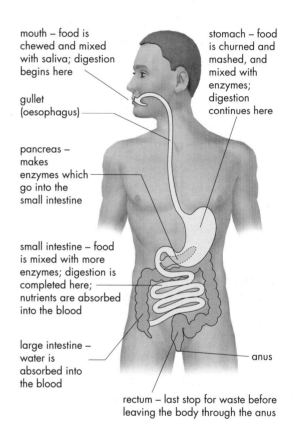

mouth – food is chewed and mixed with saliva; digestion begins here

stomach – food is churned and mashed, and mixed with enzymes; digestion continues here

gullet (oesophagus)

pancreas – makes enzymes which go into the small intestine

small intestine – food is mixed with more enzymes; digestion is completed here; nutrients are absorbed into the blood

large intestine – water is absorbed into the blood

anus

rectum – last stop for waste before leaving the body through the anus

The digestive system

a Starch, protein and fat need to be broken up because they are too big. Vitamins, minerals and water do not need to be broken up before they are absorbed. What does this suggest about the size of vitamins, minerals and water particles?

What is absorption?

Jake is eating some rice. Rice is made of starch (a carbohydrate). When he swallows, the starch moves down through his digestive system into the small intestine where the food is absorbed into the blood.

Look at the model of the small intestine. The tubing represents the walls of the small intestine and the water represents the blood outside it. The tubing has tiny holes in it (just like the wall of the digestive system). Absorption happens when the nutrients move from inside the tubing into the surrounding water.

Starch particles are too big to get through the holes. Trying to get starch through the holes is just like trying to get dried peas through the holes in a sieve.

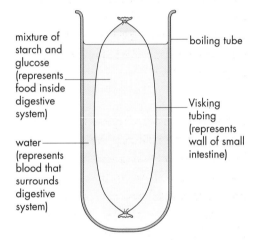

mixture of starch and glucose (represents food inside digestive system)

boiling tube

water (represents blood that surrounds digestive system)

Visking tubing (represents wall of small intestine)

ⓑ What needs to happen to the starch to make it fit through the holes in the tubing?

To be absorbed into the blood, the nutrients need to be small enough to pass through the tiny holes in the walls of the small intestine. We will look at how nutrients are made small enough for this in topic A6. In the digestive system, the wall of the small intestine is specially designed to help absorption to happen more quickly.

QUESTIONS

1 Name four parts of the digestive system.

2 a What is absorption? b What is digestion?

3 Look at the list of nutrients.
   starch   sugar   protein   fat   vitamins   minerals
   a Which of these must be digested before they can be absorbed?
   b Suggest why they need to be digested.

WHAT DO DIGESTIVE ENZYMES DO?

TOPIC CHECKLIST

- How does digestion happen?
- What do enzymes do?
- What affects enzyme action?
- Can we use enzymes commercially?

How does digestion happen?

Chewing food breaks it down into smaller pieces. Breaking food into smaller pieces is called digestion. Chewing is a type of **mechanical digestion**. It doesn't change the food into a different substance, it just breaks it into smaller pieces.

To help break down particles of starch, protein and fat, the digestive system also releases chemicals called **enzymes**. Enzymes are like very tiny scissors which break large particles into smaller particles. Because enzymes are chemicals, this is called **chemical digestion**. The smaller particles produced often have different names, because they behave like very different chemicals.

Enzyme	Where does it work?	What does it digest?	What is produced?
amylase	mouth and small intestine	starch	glucose
protease	stomach and small intestine	protein	amino acids
lipase	small intestine	fat	fatty acids and glycerol

Different enzymes are released into different parts of the digestive system. Different enzymes do different jobs. The table tells you where some of the enzymes do their jobs.

What do enzymes do?

Look at the diagram of the model small intestine on page 13. Inside the tubing there is already some starch. Starch particles are made of long chains of glucose particles joined together. Effie adds some saliva to the starch. Saliva contains **amylase enzyme** particles. These digest starch. Every time one of the enzyme particles bumps into one of these chains, the enzyme breaks another glucose particle off the end of the chain. Glucose particles are much smaller than starch particles. The starch is broken down into glucose.

But what is the point of breaking the starch down? Look at the model. The starch particles were too large to get through the holes in the Visking tubing. To absorb food through the Visking tubing, it needs to be digested. In this

a When food gets to your stomach, it gets mashed by the stomach walls. Is this mechanical or chemical digestion?

b What is the name of the group of chemicals that are responsible for chemical digestion in your body?

case, starch needs to be broken down into glucose. The glucose particles are small enough to pass through the holes in the Visking tubing. This is exactly what happens in your digestive system. After starch has been broken down into glucose in the mouth and small intestine, it can be absorbed into the bloodstream.

What affects enzyme action?

The conditions inside the digestive system can affect how quickly food is digested. Different enzymes work best in different conditions.

- Enzymes in the stomach work best in **acidic** conditions. The stomach makes hydrochloric acid to keep its enzymes working properly.

- Enzymes in the small intestine work best in **alkaline** conditions. The small intestine makes alkali to keep its enzymes working properly.

- All the enzymes in the body work best at **body temperature** (about 37 °C).

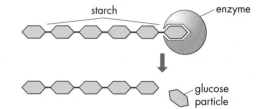

C **Food passes from the stomach into the small intestine. Suggest why enzymes from the stomach may not work properly in the small intestine.**

Can we use enzymes commercially?

Scientists have created a washing powder which contains enzymes, called biological washing powder. If enzymes can digest food inside the body, they can also digest dirt or food when it is stuck on clothes. Biological washing powder has the advantage that you can wash clothes at a lower temperature because the enzymes in the powder work best at around 40 °C. Normally you need very hot water to get very dirty clothes clean.

Some people are allergic to the enzymes in washing powder, and they must use non-biological washing powder instead.

Different types of washing powder

QUESTIONS

1 What is the difference between mechanical and chemical digestion?

2 Describe what enzymes do.

3 Write down two conditions within the gut that can affect how quickly food is digested.

WHERE ARE THE PRODUCTS OF DIGESTION USED?

TOPIC CHECKLIST

- How are nutrients transported around the body?
- How are the nutrients used?
- What happens to food that cannot be digested?
- What happens to water?

How are nutrients transported around the body?

Nutrients are absorbed into the **blood** in the small intestine. The blood is a bit like the postal service in the body. It sweeps the nutrients away from the digestive system and delivers them to cells all around the body. You will learn more about how this happens in Unit B.

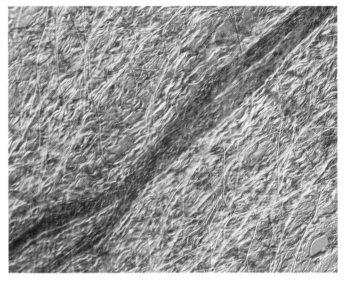

Blood flowing past cells in your body

How are the nutrients used?

As we saw in topic A1, each type of nutrient is needed by the rest of the body for a particular reason. For example:

- Proteins are needed for growth and repair. If you damage part of your body, proteins are used to mend it again.

- Carbohydrates, like glucose, are needed for energy, particularly in your muscle cells. Be careful though, if more glucose is absorbed than you can use, the extra glucose is stored as fat. That is why eating too many sweet things may make you overweight.

Ⓐ **To which part of the body does blood carry vitamin C?**

What happens to food that cannot be digested?

Fibre cannot be digested. This is because our bodies do not make an enzyme to digest it. Fruit, vegetables and cereals contain fibre. Grass is almost completely made of fibre. Cows and horses have the right enzymes to digest grass but we don't. Because we cannot digest it, we do not bother eating it.

These are all high-fibre foods

Because fibre cannot be digested, it cannot be absorbed into the bloodstream. As a result, it passes through the digestive system and is **egested** (pushed out) from the body through the **anus** as part of the **faeces** (waste material). Because it is not absorbed into the bloodstream to be used by the body's cells, most people do not think of fibre as a nutrient.

Having said that, it is very important that we eat fibre because it helps keep food moving through our digestive system. Food only moves through the digestive system because of muscles pushing on it. Fibre helps this happen in two ways:

- It absorbs some water, keeping the food moist. Imagine if all the food dried out inside the digestive system. It might get stuck halfway down!

- It gives the muscles in the digestive system something to push on. Food only moves along because muscles push it. Most digested food dissolves in water. Fibre is not digested and stays solid. This helps the muscles to push it through the digestive system.

What happens to water?

Although water is needed to keep food moving through your digestive system, it is also important not to lose too much water in the faeces. For one thing, it would give you diarrhoea, which is rather unpleasant! More importantly, your body needs water inside its cells and body fluids. Because of this, water is absorbed into the blood in the large intestine. If, having absorbed it into the blood, the body has too much water, it gets rid of the extra through the urine.

QUESTIONS

1 How are nutrients transported from the digestive system to the rest of the cells in your body?

2 If fibre is not absorbed, why do we need to eat it?

3 What happens to water after you drink it?

B Respiration

WHAT HAPPENS TO FOOD MOLECULES AFTER DIGESTION?

TOPIC CHECKLIST

- What does your body do with food?
- How is glucose used by your body?
- How do cells release energy from glucose?
- What else does aerobic respiration produce?

What does your body do with food?

In Unit A, you saw how starch particles are made of long chains of glucose. Each glucose is broken off the end of the chain by digestion. After digestion the glucose is absorbed into the blood. Glucose is carried around your body by the blood. All of the cells in your body need glucose for energy. In this unit, we will see how your cells release the energy from glucose.

How is glucose used by your body?

High-energy drinks, like the one on the right, is glucose. Glucose is found in many different types of food. It is a store of energy. The energy needs to be released from the glucose by your cells.

(a) **Explain why athletes often use high-energy drinks.**

Blood flows all around the body to deliver glucose to all the body's cells. Some cells, like muscle cells and brain cells, need more glucose than others. This is because they work hard and need more energy than other cells.

How do cells release energy from glucose?

If you burn fuel in oxygen, energy is released. We often burn fuels to get energy. This is the equation for burning fuel.

$$\textit{fuel} + \textit{oxygen} \rightarrow \textit{carbon dioxide} + \textit{water} + \textit{energy}$$

A high energy drink

We use fuel for energy

We can also burn food to give us energy. Look at the piece of burning biscuit; it is reacting with the oxygen in the air.

b **Which two types of energy are being released from the burning biscuit?**

In humans, energy is not released from food by burning, but by a similar reaction called **aerobic respiration**. Glucose from the food reacts with oxygen to release energy. Instead of all the energy being released suddenly as light and heat, most energy is released in a much more controlled way as chemical energy. A small amount of energy is released slowly as heat.

Look at Julia. By breathing on the thermometer, she has made the temperature rise. Her body is releasing heat energy. All the energy released by Julia originally comes from her food.

Biscuits release energy as well

What else does aerobic respiration produce?

Respiration does not just release energy. Look again at the equation for burning. As well as energy, burning produces water and carbon dioxide. Aerobic respiration in human cells is very similar – it also produces water and carbon dioxide.

c **You get rid of a lot of the water made in respiration several times a day. Where do you go to do this?**

d **Lime-water goes cloudy when you bubble carbon dioxide through it. The picture shows what happens when Julia breathes out into the lime-water. What does this tell us about the air she breathes out?**

The equation for respiration is very similar to the equation for burning. Respiration happens in every cell of your body.

glucose + oxygen → carbon dioxide + water + energy

Humans produce heat

Humans produce carbon dioxide

QUESTIONS

1 Why does your body need glucose?

2 How does glucose normally enter your blood?

3 Explain why **a** muscle cells and **b** brain cells need a lot of energy.

4 What gas is needed for aerobic respiration to happen?

5 What gas is produced by aerobic respiration?

HOW DOES OXYGEN GET INTO THE BLOOD?

TOPIC CHECKLIST

- What happens in your lungs?
- Where does gaseous exchange happen?
- Why are alveoli good at their job?
- What happens if your lungs get damaged?

What happens in your lungs?

Your cells use oxygen in respiration. When you breathe air into the lungs (**inhale** or **inspire**), oxygen passes into your blood. Blood carries oxygen from the lungs to all your cells.

Your cells make carbon dioxide during respiration. Blood carries carbon dioxide from your cells to the lungs. Carbon dioxide leaves your blood in the lungs and is then breathed out (**exhaled** or **expired**).

The air you breathe in (inhaled air) and the air your breathe out (exhaled air) contain different amounts of different gases.

Gas	Inhaled air	Exhaled air
oxygen	21%	16%
carbon dioxide	0.03%	4%
nitrogen	79%	79%
water vapour	variable level	high level

ⓐ Why does exhaled air have more carbon dioxide than inhaled air?

ⓑ Which of the gases in the table is not used by the body?

Where does gaseous exchange happen?

Look at the diagram of a person's chest. When you breathe in, air flows down your trachea. The trachea splits into two tubes called bronchi (each one is called a bronchus). Each bronchus splits into lots of very small tubes called bronchioles. At the ends of the bronchioles the air reaches tiny sacs called **alveoli**. The alveoli are surrounded by lots of **capillaries**. Capillaries are small tubes which bring and carry away blood.

ⓒ **Draw a flow chart showing the pathway of air into the lungs.**

Oxygen passes into the blood from the air in the alveoli. Carbon dioxide passes into the alveoli from the blood. This is called **gaseous exchange**.

- When blood from the body arrives at an alveolus, it contains very little oxygen. Most of the oxygen has been used up by body cells in respiration. Because there is so little oxygen in the blood and so much in the alveolus, oxygen moves from the alveolus into the blood.

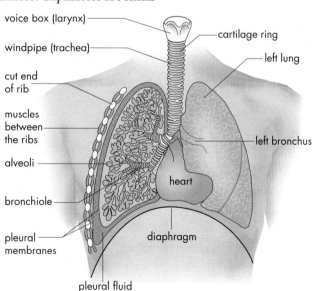

voice box (larynx) —
windpipe (trachea) —
cut end of rib —
muscles between the ribs —
alveoli —
bronchiole —
pleural membranes —
pleural fluid —
cartilage ring —
left lung —
left bronchus —
heart —
diaphragm —

- When blood from the body arrives at an alveolus, it contains a lot of carbon dioxide. This is produced by the body cells in respiration. Because there is so much carbon dioxide in the blood, and so little in the alveolus, carbon dioxide moves into the alveolus from the blood.

Why are alveoli good at their job?

Because there are so many alveoli inside the lungs, they provide an enormous surface area for gases to get in and out of the blood. If you unwrapped all the alveoli in your lungs and flattened them out, they would have a total area larger than a tennis court!

d **Why is it important for the lungs to have a big surface area?**

The alveoli don't just provide a big surface area. They also have special features (**adaptations**), which allow gases to get in and out of the blood more easily.

- **Thin walls (one cell thick)**: Oxygen and carbon dioxide can squeeze easily through the walls into and out of the blood.

- **Good blood supply**: The oxygen is carried away from the lungs quickly and the carbon dioxide arrives at the lungs quickly.

- **Moist lining**: To get through the walls, the gases must be dissolved in water. The moist lining is there to help them dissolve.

What happens if your lungs get damaged?

Picture **A** is of a healthy person's lungs. Picture **B** is of the lungs of someone with emphysema. Emphysema is a disease which can be caused by smoking, and which makes the alveoli burst.

Because people with emphysema have fewer alveoli, less oxygen can be absorbed into the blood. As a result of this, less oxygen goes into the blood during each breath. This means that emphysema sufferers have to breathe faster to get the same amount of oxygen as someone who has healthy lungs. This makes them short of breath and lacking in energy.

QUESTIONS

1 Which contains more oxygen – inhaled air or exhaled air?

2 What is gaseous exchange?

3 Why do the alveoli need to be moist?

4 Why do people with emphysema get short of breath?

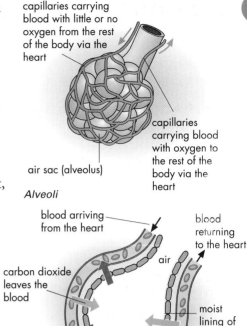

Alveoli

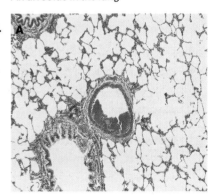

An alveolus in the lung

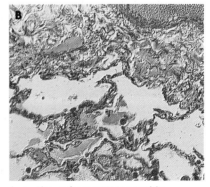

Healthy lung tissue

Lung tissue from someone with emphysema

HOW DO OXYGEN AND GLUCOSE REACH THE CELLS?

TOPIC CHECKLIST

● What does your blood do?

● What happens when blood reaches your cells?

What does your blood do?

Your blood is made of a liquid called **plasma**, and two types of cells: **red blood cells** and **white blood cells**.

Your blood carries oxygen and glucose to your body's cells for respiration. It also takes carbon dioxide and water away from the cells when they are produced by respiration.

Before respiration

● Glucose enters your body through the digestive system. Glucose is carried from the digestive system to your body's cells by the plasma in the blood.

● Oxygen enters your body through the lungs. Oxygen is carried from the lungs to your body's cells by the red blood cells in the blood.

ⓐ **Draw a flow chart to describe the route glucose takes from your mouth to a leg muscle cell.**

ⓑ **Draw a flow chart to describe the route oxygen takes from your mouth to a leg muscle cell.**

After respiration

● Carbon dioxide is carried away from your body's cells to your lungs by the plasma in the blood. Carbon dioxide leaves your body when you breathe out.

● Water is carried away from your body's cells to your kidneys by the plasma in the blood. Water leaves your body when your kidneys make urine.

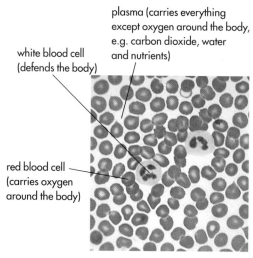

plasma (carries everything except oxygen around the body, e.g. carbon dioxide, water and nutrients)

white blood cell (defends the body)

red blood cell (carries oxygen around the body)

Blood cells

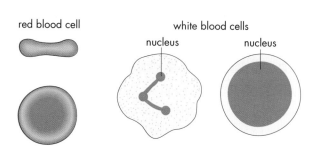

red blood cell

white blood cells

nucleus

nucleus

What happens when blood reaches your cells?

Blood always passes through the heart on its journey around the body. The heart pumps the blood around the body. It travels in tubes called blood vessels. Blood is carried to your cells in very small blood vessels called capillaries, which have very thin walls. This makes it easy for oxygen and glucose to get through the walls of the capillaries, and to go to cells where they are needed for respiration. It is also easy for the carbon dioxide and water from respiration to get out of the cells and into the capillaries.

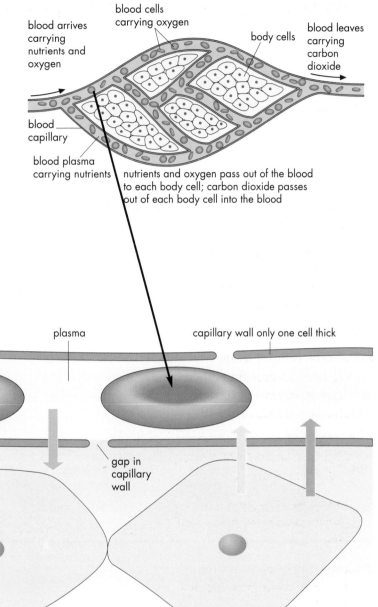

blood cells carrying oxygen

blood arrives carrying nutrients and oxygen

body cells

blood leaves carrying carbon dioxide

blood capillary

blood plasma carrying nutrients

nutrients and oxygen pass out of the blood to each body cell; carbon dioxide passes out of each body cell into the blood

red blood cell

plasma

capillary wall only one cell thick

gap in capillary wall

body cell

Key — oxygen — water — carbon dioxide — glucose

QUESTIONS

1 Which part of the blood carries **a** glucose and **b** oxygen around your body?

2 Where do **a** oxygen and **b** glucose enter the body?

3 Where do **a** carbon dioxide and **b** water leave the body?

4 Why do capillaries have thin walls?

- How does the heart work?
- What happens if your blood cannot supply enough glucose and oxygen to your cells?

How does the heart work?

The heart pumps blood around your body. Blood flows through a network of tubes called blood vessels. There are three types of blood vessels.

- **Arteries** carry blood away from the heart.
- **Veins** carry blood towards the heart.
- **Capillaries** carry blood between the arteries and the veins.

The walls of the heart are made of muscle. The muscles in the walls of the right and left ventricles squeeze blood out of the heart through the arteries. Arteries have strong, thick walls because blood is squirted through them at high pressure. When the blood returns to the heart after travelling around the body or travelling back from the lungs, it travels through veins that enter the left and right atria (plural of atrium). Look carefully at the diagram of the circulation. The blood leaves the right ventricle of the heart, goes to the lungs, and comes back. Only then is it pumped around the rest of the body by the left ventricle.

Because of this, people call the heart a **double pump**. The right-hand side pumps blood to the lungs; the left-hand side pumps blood to the rest of the body.

a Why does the left ventricle have a thicker layer of muscle than the right ventricle?

b Describe the path of a red blood cell around the body from the moment it picks up oxygen in the lungs.

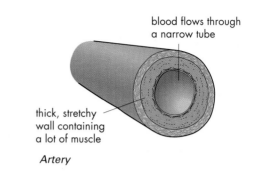

blood flows through a narrow tube

thick, stretchy wall containing a lot of muscle

Artery

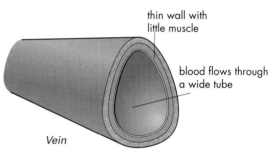

thin wall with little muscle

blood flows through a wide tube

Vein

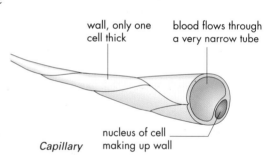

wall, only one cell thick

blood flows through a very narrow tube

nucleus of cell making up wall

Capillary

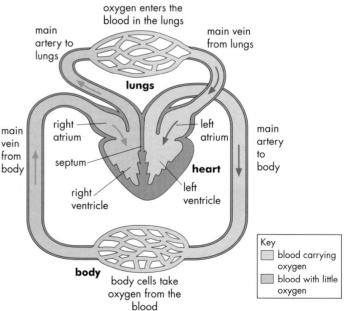

oxygen enters the blood in the lungs

main artery to lungs

main vein from lungs

lungs

main vein from body

right atrium

left atrium

main artery to body

septum

heart

right ventricle

left ventricle

body

body cells take oxygen from the blood

Key
☐ blood carrying oxygen
☐ blood with little oxygen

Your circulation

What happens if your blood cannot supply enough glucose and oxygen to your cells?

If your heart is faulty, it doesn't pump blood very quickly. This means your cells don't get oxygen and glucose very quickly. If they don't get enough oxygen and glucose, they can't release as much energy. But even if your heart is working normally, sometimes your cells need so much oxygen and glucose that your heart can't beat quickly enough to supply them.

If you do a lot of exercise, your cells need a lot of energy, and therefore need a lot of oxygen and glucose. During exercise, your heart beats faster to speed up the supply of glucose and oxygen to your cells. However, during intense exercise, your heart cannot supply your cells quickly enough to release all the energy they need.

In B1, we talked about aerobic respiration. Aerobic means 'with oxygen', so aerobic respiration is respiration using oxygen. During intense exercise, your cells start to do a different type of respiration: **anaerobic respiration** (respiration without oxygen). Anaerobic respiration releases less energy and makes a chemical called **lactic acid**. This makes your muscles ache.

It is not just during exercise that your cells don't get enough oxygen. Illness and high altitude can also reduce the oxygen supply to your cells.

A runner at the end of a race

Walking at high altitudes can reduce your oxygen supply

QUESTIONS

1 Why do people say that the heart is a 'double pump'?

2 a What is anaerobic respiration?

   b When does anaerobic respiration happen?

   c What is produced by anaerobic respiration?

3 When someone has a heart attack, their heart can stop. Explain why this can put their life in danger.

WHO UNRAVELLED THE MYSTERIES OF CIRCULATION?

- What did researchers find out about circulation?
- What did Harvey find out about circulation?

What did researchers find out about circulation?

People have been studying the blood system for over 2000 years! Read the stories to find out how.

Galen, a Greek doctor

Galen was a Greek doctor in the 13th century who spent a lot of his life treating Roman Emperors. He had quite a few ideas about the blood:

- Blood is carried around the body in arteries and veins.

- Blood is made in the liver, mixed in the brain and the lungs with a substance called 'spirit' and then used up around the body.

- Blood goes from one side of the heart to the other through tiny holes in the middle.

ⓐ Which of these ideas do you think is right?

Over the years, different researchers proved some of his ideas to be wrong.

Ibn an-Nafis and the lungs

Ibn an-Nafis worked in Cairo in 1242. He disagreed with Galen about movement of blood in the heart. He thought that blood went through the lungs. Because his religion would not let him dissect human bodies, he could not prove his theory.

da Vinci, the Italian artist

Leonardo da Vinci did prove that blood passed through the lungs in the 15th century by dissecting and drawing lots of human bodies. Unfortunately though, da Vinci did not publish his results; they were only discovered in his private notebooks years later.

Vesalius, Columbo and Fabricius

In 1543, Andreas Vesalius realised that Galen had made another mistake. Vesalius was Professor of Anatomy at the University of Padua in Italy. By dissecting human bodies, he realised that there were no holes linking the two sides of the heart. But if there were no holes in the septum, how did blood move within the heart? Realdo Columbo, who became Professor at Padua after Vesalius, suggested that blood went from the heart to the lungs in the arteries, through the lungs, and back from the lungs to the heart in the veins. Fabricius, the next Professor at Padua, discovered that veins had valves, which stopped blood flowing backwards.

What did Harvey find out about circulation?

After all these researchers' work, it was left to someone to put everybody's ideas together into a combined theory. That was William Harvey. He worked out exactly how blood travels around the body. He published his results in 1628 in a book '*On the movement of the heart and blood in animals*'.

- He looked at the valves and muscles of the heart, and realised that the heart pumped blood around the body.

- He measured how much blood was pumped by one heartbeat, and calculated the total amount pumped every hour. Remember that Galen thought that blood was made in the liver from the food we eat. Harvey realised that the heart pumped more blood every hour, than could possibly be made by the liver in that time. This meant that blood must be pumped around the body over and over again. In other words blood circulates around the body.

- He tried to push liquids the wrong way, and worked out that blood only travels in one direction in each type of blood vessel.

There was one problem with Harvey's theory. The arteries carrying blood away from the heart got smaller and smaller until they could not be seen. The veins also 'disappeared'. Although he could not prove it, he predicted that the arteries and veins were linked by tiny blood vessels.

ⓑ **What is the name for the tiny blood vessels which Harvey thought must link arteries and veins?**

1

Swellings show the position of the valves.

2

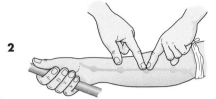

Block the vein by pushing with the fingers.

3

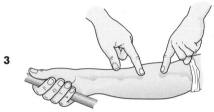

Leave the left finger in place and push blood to the left swelling with the right finger

4

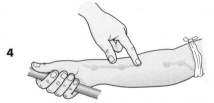

Take the left finger away.
The blood will not flow back.

5

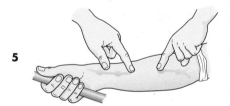

The blood won't even flow back if you try pushing with the right finger.

Harvey's famous experiment

QUESTIONS

1 Summarise what the following researchers said about the blood:
   a Galen
   b Vesalius
   c da Vinci
   d Harvey.

2 What is the evidence that blood cannot go directly from one side of the heart to the other?

DO OTHER LIVING THINGS RESPIRE?

Do other animals respire?

As we saw in topic B1, humans respire to release energy from their food. Other animals also need to respire to get energy from the food they eat. If other animals do respire, we would expect them to produce carbon dioxide, water and energy, and to use up oxygen. You can investigate this using the experiments below.

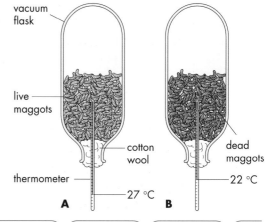

Do animals release energy?

Look at the picture of the vacuum flasks. Flask **A** contains living maggots. Flask **B** contains dead maggots.

ⓐ **Look at the thermometers. Do living animals release heat energy?**

Do animals produce carbon dioxide?

Look at the picture of the experiment to test if animals produce carbon dioxide. Air is sucked through the apparatus from left to right. The air that enters the animal's chamber does not contain any carbon dioxide.

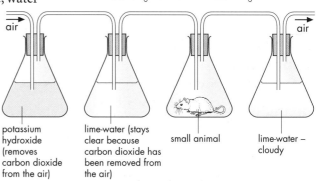

Do animals produce carbon dioxide?

ⓑ **Does the air leaving the animal's chamber contain carbon dioxide?**

ⓒ **Do animals produce carbon dioxide?**

Do animals produce water?

Look at the dog. Decide for yourself whether animals produce water!

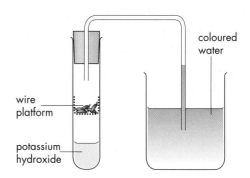

Do animals produce water?

Do animals use up oxygen?

Look at the diagram. If animals use up oxygen, you would expect them to take it out of the air in the tube. If they do, the water should move up the tube to fill the space that is left. You can see that this has happened, and that animals do use up oxygen.

Do animals use oxygen?

Do plants respire?

Plants are just like animals – they respire in exactly the same way. Plants use up oxygen and produce carbon dioxide, water and energy. You can show this using the experiments below.

Do plants release energy?

Look at the picture of the peas opposite. The peas in flask A are living. The peas in flask B have been killed by boiling them in water.

The flask with the living peas is hotter than the flask with the dead peas. The living peas are releasing energy in the form of heat. That energy is being released by respiration. The dead peas cannot respire.

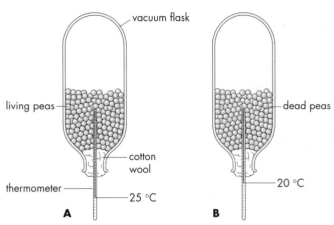

Do plants release energy?

Do plants produce carbon dioxide and use up oxygen?

You can use the same experiments as those shown for animals here. However, you must do the experiments in the dark. This does not mean that plants only respire at night; they are doing it all the time. However, during the day the carbon dioxide, which is produced by respiration, is used up immediately by the plant in a process called photosynthesis. Likewise, during the day, the plant produces extra oxygen in the same process. You will learn more about photosynthesis in year 9.

Do plants produce water?

Look at the photograph of the plant in the plastic bag. It has been left like this for 24 hours. You can see tiny droplets of water on the inside of the bag. These have been released by the plant during respiration.

Do plants produce water?

QUESTIONS

1 What chemical turns cloudy in the presence of carbon dioxide?

2 In the experiment showing that animals use up oxygen, there is some potassium hydroxide in the tube. What does this do?

3 For plants, you have to do respiration experiments in the dark. Explain why.

C Microbes and disease

WHAT ARE MICROORGANISMS?

TOPIC CHECKLIST

● What do microorganisms do?

● What do microorganisms look like?

What do microorganisms do?

Microorganisms (**microbes**) are tiny living things. They are so small, you need a microscope to see them. They share the same features as other living things:

● They need food to use in respiration for energy.

● They grow.

● They reproduce. Because some of them are made only of one cell, they can reproduce simply by cell division.

ⓐ **To survive, microbes need the same conditions as you or I. One condition that we need is a constant supply of food. Name two other conditions that microbes may need in order to survive.**

People are interested in microbes because they can cause disease in humans, animals and plants. They can also make food and drink **rot** (go bad).

To stop the unwanted effects of microbes, people use chemicals to kill them. These chemicals include disinfectants, antiseptics and bleach.

People are also interested in microbes because they can be useful. Some can be used to make food, some can be eaten as food, and some can even make medicines to help cure disease.

What do microorganisms look like?

The table opposite summarises the three main types of microbes: viruses, bacteria and fungi.

ⓑ **Which is the smallest type of microbe?**

ⓒ **Which microbes are made of living cells?**

ⓓ **Why can microbes make you ill?**

Mould growing on food

Chemicals that kill microbes

Microbes are used to make bread, wine and yoghurt

Medicines can kill bacteria that have made you ill

	Viruses	Bacteria	Fungi
What they look like	genetic information — protein coat	cell wall, cell membrane, cytoplasm, genetic information (not in a nucleus)	yeast, pin-mould, mushroom
Size	viruses are tiny – their length is only about one millionth of a millimetre	bacteria are larger than viruses – their length is around one thousandth of a millimetre	fungi can be very small or very large – the yeast can be seen only with a microscope because it is so small
Structure	a strand of genetic information surrounded by a protein coat	living cells containing cytoplasm and a loop of genetic information, surrounded by a cell wall	lots of living cells with nuclei and cell walls, joined together in long strands called hyphae
How harmful types can make you ill	release poisons; invade tissues and take over cells, making millions of copies of themselves inside the cells	multiply quickly to make lots of bacteria – each one can release posions which can attack your cells	grow quickly, releasing poisons which can attack your cells
Uses	none	used to make yoghurt	make antibiotics (medicines); used in making bread, wine and beer

QUESTIONS

1 What are the three types of microorganism?

2 What are **a** viruses, **b** bacteria and **c** fungi made of?

3 a Write down two uses of microbes.

b Give two examples of microbes being harmful.

HOW CAN WE USE MICROBES?

TOPIC CHECKLIST

- How are microbes grown to make food?
- How are microbes grown in the laboratory?

How are microbes grown to make food?

Bread

Yeast is a fungus. It is used in making bread along with flour, water, sugar and fat. Once mixed with warm water and sugar, each yeast cell starts to reproduce and makes the dough rise.

In Unit B, you learnt that all organisms respire. They do this to release energy from their food. For yeast cells, the food is the sugar in the bread mixture. The yeast makes carbon dioxide when it respires. The bread rises because the yeast makes bubbles of carbon dioxide gas inside the bread. Yeast will only grow properly at the correct temperature. If it is too hot, the yeast will die. If it is too cold, the yeast will not reproduce, and there will be very few yeast cells making carbon dioxide.

ⓐ **What conditions does yeast need to grow and respire?**

ⓑ **Apart from carbon dioxide, what else is produced when respiration happens?**

Yoghurt

Certain bacteria can change milk into yoghurt. Two different bacteria are added to the milk. When mixed with the milk, they turn a sugar called lactose into an acid called lactic acid. This process is called **fermentation**:

lactose + water → lactic acid

The lactic acid makes the protein particles in the milk stick together. When this happens, the milk gets thicker and becomes yoghurt.

The best temperature for this to happen is 46 °C. At this temperature, the bacteria reproduce quickly, and so more fermentation happens. This means more yoghurt is produced more quickly.

ⓒ **What do you think will happen if the temperature is too hot or too cold for the bacteria?**

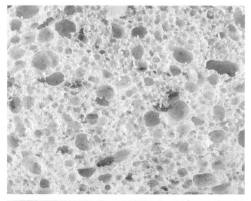

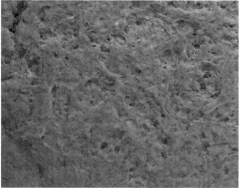

Making bread

Making yoghurt

How are microbes grown in the laboratory?

We can grow microbes in the lab by using a Petri dish containing a layer of agar (an 'agar plate'). Agar is a special jelly which provides good conditions for bacteria and fungi to grow and which contains all the food they need to survive.

Imagine you are a doctor and your patient has food poisoning. Food poisoning is caused by microbes. You suspect that the fish paste, which your patient ate yesterday, contains microbes. You need to know which microbe is in the fish paste before you can treat your patient. To find out, you must grow the microbe until there is enough for you to recognise it. You can do this by following the steps described below.

1 Sterilise a wire loop by dipping it in ethanol and heating it in a blue Bunsen burner flame. Make sure you keep the ethanol well away from the Bunsen burner. Ethanol is very flammable (it sets on fire easily).

2 Let the loop cool down and dip it in the fish paste.

3 Take the lid off the Petri dish and spread the fish paste in clear lines across the agar.

4 Put the lid back on the Petri dish immediately to stop other microbes getting in.

5 Tape up the Petri dish to stop anyone opening it. Microbes can cause disease.

6 Leave the petri dish in a warm place, upside down to stop water collecting on the surface of the agar.

7 Keep checking it every few days. Never open the Petri dish to look at the microbes; just look through the plastic.

d **Why should you let the loop cool down before dipping it in the fish paste?**

QUESTIONS

1 Why does yeast need sugar in order to make the bread rise?

2 Why does it need to be warm in order to make yoghurt?

3 a Write down two safety precautions you should take when growing microbes on agar plates.

   b Explain why you need to take each of these precautions.

An agar plate

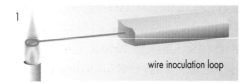

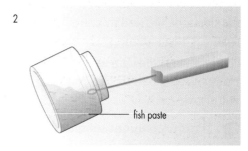

wire inoculation loop

fish paste

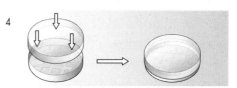

lines of paste spread onto agar

Petri dish

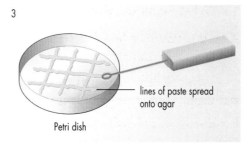

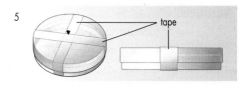

tape

Growing microbes from fish paste

CAN MICROBES BE HARMFUL?

TOPIC CHECKLIST

- What is infection?
- What causes infection?
- How can microbes enter your body?
- How can you avoid infection?

What is infection?

Look at the woman in the picture. She has a cold. Colds are normally caused by viruses. When the woman sneezes, she sprays lots of tiny water droplets into the air. These droplets may contain viruses. If you are close to the woman when she sneezes, and breathe in any of these droplets, you could also catch a cold.

The woman's cold is an **infection**. She is **infectious**, which means she can pass the infection on to you. If the virus enters your body, you have been infected with that virus.

(a) **What precautions should someone with a cold to take to stop them spreading the infection?**

What causes infection?

It is not just viruses that can make you ill. Bacteria and fungi can also cause disease. Any organism that causes a disease is called a **pathogen**. Look at the table below to see which microbes cause which illnesses.

A small number of illnesses are also caused by single-celled animals called protozoans. These are not viruses, bacteria or fungi. Malaria is caused by a protozoan called *Plasmodium*. It is carried by an insect called a mosquito and passed on when it bites different people.

Viruses	Bacteria	Fungi
colds	meningitis	athlete's foot
flu	food poisoning	thrush
tetanus	tuberculosis	
measles	typhoid	
chicken pox	whooping cough	
AIDS		

How can microbes enter your body?

For infection to happen, a microbe must be **transmitted** from one person to another. You saw how the cold virus can be transmitted when microbes in water droplets are inhaled. Microbes can also be transmitted by

- eating infected food or drinking unclean water
- breathing in air containing microbes
- allowing microbes to get into the blood through cuts and grazes.

A fetus inside a pregnant mother's uterus can also catch some diseases from its mother. This happens when microbes go across the placenta from the mother's blood to the fetus' blood. German measles (*Rubella*) is a good example of this. A baby may also catch a disease from drinking its mother's milk.

It is also possible to be infected with some microbes during sexual intercourse. These microbes cause **sexually transmitted diseases**. An example is AIDS.

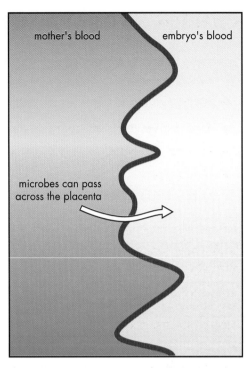

Inside the placenta

How can you avoid infection?

Different microbes enter your body in different ways. The way to avoid infection depends on the microbe, and how it enters your body:

1 Cook food thoroughly. Cooking food kills microbes because they cannot survive at high temperatures.

2 Wash your hands after going to the toilet. Bacteria on the fingers can easily get onto food.

3 Avoid drinking or bathing in infected water. Always drink purified water (purified water comes out of the tap in Britain).

4 Avoid sharing drinks with other people as they may be infected.

5 Use insect repellent to keep infective insects away.

6 Wash cuts thoroughly and cover them while they heal.

7 Always use a condom during sexual intercourse.

b **Why should you make sure your food is properly cooked before eating it?**

QUESTIONS

1 Explain what infection means.

2 Give one disease caused by
a a bacterium, **b** a virus,
c a fungus, **d** a protozoan.

3 List four ways in which microbes can enter your body.

4 Imagine you are a virus that causes the flu. Explain how you are transmitted from one person to another.

STOPPING THE SPREAD OF DISEASE

TOPIC CHECKLIST

- How do you stop diseases spreading?
- Who is involved in stopping diseases spreading

How do you stop diseases spreading?

If a disease spreads quickly and infects a lot of people, we say there is an epidemic of that disease. The three passages below describe how people have tried to stop the spread of disease.

The Great Plague

During the Great Plague in the 17th century, lots of people died in London, but people in the countryside stayed healthy. One day, in the village of Eyam in Derbyshire, a parcel arrived from London. In the bottom of the parcel were some old, damp cloths. The tailor who unwrapped the parcel died a few days after handling these cloths, and the plague then spread around the village. Many people wanted to leave the village to avoid the plague, but the vicar told them not to. He realised that if they went to other villages, the plague would spread there as well. The village was isolated for months and over 250 people died from plague. However, because nobody had been

allowed to leave the village, the spread of plague into the rest of the countryside was stopped.

a **How did the vicar stop the plague spreading?**

Cholera

In 1854, cholera broke out in the Broad Street area of London. Most doctors thought the disease was spread through the air. Dr John Snow disagreed. He decided that the disease was transmitted through drinking polluted water. He used four pieces of evidence to reach his conclusion:

1 People with cholera had all drunk water from the same well. People who drank water from other wells did not catch the disease.

2 Workers in a local brewery who drank beer rather than water all day did not catch the disease!

3 A woman in Hampstead (an area free of cholera) had a large bottle of Broad Street water sent over every day. She was the only woman in Hampstead to die of cholera.

4 When John Snow stopped people using the Broad Street well, the cholera outbreak quickly cleared up.

b **What did John Snow do to stop the cholera spreading?**

Yellow fever

In 1881, Dr Carlos Finlay from Havana, Cuba suggested that mosquitoes transmitted yellow fever from person to person. In 1900, Dr. Walter Reed, an American army doctor, tested this. He used two groups of very brave volunteers.

- The first group slept on the clothes of people with yellow fever. Mosquitoes were kept away and none of these people caught yellow fever.

- The second group were kept away from sick people. Mosquitoes which had bitten people with yellow fever were allowed to bite the volunteers. Many of them caught yellow fever.

Dr Reed was convinced that mosquitoes spread yellow fever. He destroyed the wet breeding grounds of the mosquitoes outside the city. Havana became free of yellow fever for the first time in over 150 years.

c **How did Dr. Reed stop yellow fever spreading?**

A malarial swamp

Who is involved in stopping diseases spreading?

If a disease breaks out now, lots of different people and organisations are involved in controlling its spread. Look at the two case histories below. Try to decide which of the people in the spider diagram would be needed to control the outbreaks of *Escherichia coli* and *Ebola*.

Teachers tell people how to stop disease spreading

Police stop people moving around the country and spreading disease

Doctors diagnose and treat the disease

dealing with an outbreak of disease

Public Health Officers shut down food shops which are the source of disease

Health workers clean infected areas and deal with infected people who have died

Nurses look after the sufferers

Anyone treating Ebola patients should wear gloves, masks and protective coats

Lots of different people are involved in stopping the spread of disease

Case history 1

In the late 1990s, many people in Scotland died from food poisoning. This broke out because people had bought contaminated meat from a butcher. The meat was contaminated with a bacterium called *Escherichia coli*.

Case history 2

Ebola is a disease caused by a virus. It destroys the body by making it bleed, both inside and outside. A serious outbreak happened in 1995 in Kikwit, Zaire. The virus spreads in body fluids. Any contact with an infected person's blood is very dangerous.

QUESTIONS

1 Give three ways of stopping diseases being transmitted.

2 a Write down three different people who may be involved in stopping a disease spreading.

  b Explain how each of them helps to control the disease.

PROTECTION AGAINST DISEASE: NATURAL DEFENCES

TOPIC CHECKLIST

- What stops microbes getting into your body?
- What happens if microbes get into your body?
- What else can make you ill?

What stops microbes getting into your body?

Our environment contains a lot of microbes, many of which can cause disease. Our bodies need to defend us against these microbes, otherwise we would be ill most of the time. The **skin** is the main barrier against microbes, although the body also has other ways of stopping microbes getting in:

- the nose has hairs to catch microbes

- the nose and windpipe are lined with a sticky substance, mucus, which microbes get stuck to on their way into the body

- the eyes make tears which wash microbes away from the eyes.

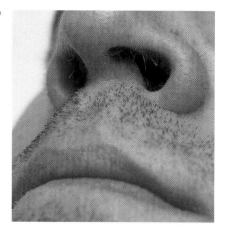

What happens if microbes get into your body?

Sometimes microbes manage to avoid all these barriers.
If this happens, and microbes get inside your body, there are two types of **white blood cells** which are ready to defend you.

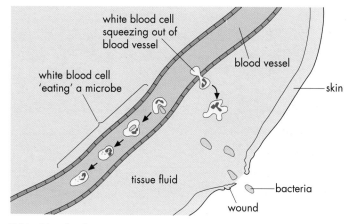

White blood cells

Eating microbes

Some white blood cells 'eat' and destroy microbes. When you cut your skin, white blood cells move to the cut to eat microbes that have got into your blood. The white blood cells can even squeeze out of the blood vessels to 'hunt down' microbes that have not yet reached the blood.

Making antibodies

Some white blood cells make **antibodies** that help to destroy microbes. Each microbe needs a different antibody to destroy it. Each different antibody is produced by a different set of white blood cells. Antibodies can help destroy microbes in three ways.

- Some antibodies are like missiles. They puncture holes in the microbes, killing them directly.

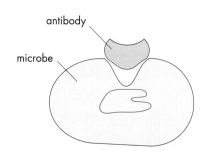

- Some antibodies are like glue. They stick big groups of microbes together, helping other white blood cells to find them and 'eat' them more easily.

- Some antibodies are like policemen. They surround and stick to the microbe, making it harmless.

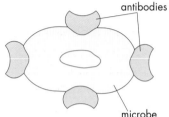

Young children are sometimes less resistant to microbes than older children. This is because older children have had more time to make antibodies to particular microbes. Elderly people also have less effective defence against disease. This is because they do not produce enough white blood cells.

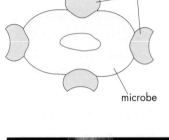

What else can make you ill?

Infectious diseases only happen if you are infected with a microbe. However, microbes are not the only things that can make you ill.

Some people in the world are ill because they have not been able to eat enough food, or because they have not eaten a balanced diet with all the nutrients their body needs.

- People who do not eat enough fruit may get **scurvy**. This is because they do not get enough vitamin C. People with scurvy have soft gums and skin, and their teeth often fall out! There is a photo of scurvy in topic A2.

- People who do not eat enough vitamin D suffer from **rickets**. People with rickets have soft bones which bend easily. You can increase the amount of vitamin D in your diet by drinking more milk or eating more fish.

Other people are ill because they have inherited a disease from their parents. When someone has an inherited disease, there is normally a problem with the instructions inside the nucleus of each of their cells.

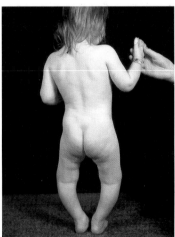

A child with rickets

- **Cystic fibrosis** is a disease which stops people breathing properly. This is because they make too much mucus in their windpipe.

- **Sickle-cell anaemia** is a disease which stops a person's blood carrying oxygen properly. It makes the blood cells into 'half-moon' shapes which get clogged up with each other in the capillaries.

QUESTIONS

1 Write down three ways in which your body stops microbes getting into your blood.

2 Give two ways in which white blood cells destroy microbes.

3 How do antibodies help destroy microbes?

4 Illnesses are not always caused by microbes. Name two other reasons why people may become ill.

PROTECTION AGAINST DISEASE: ANTIBIOTICS

TOPIC CHECKLIST

- How do scientists help us fight disease?
- What are antibiotics?
- Can antibiotics cure diseases cased by viruses?
- What are the problems with antibiotics?

How do scientists help us fight disease?

Disease happens when a particular type of microbe enters your blood for the first time. The microbe makes you ill until your white blood cells have made enough antibodies to kill it off. This may take some time, and in some cases the microbe may have caused serious illness or even death before this happens.

To help us avoid the dangers of infections, scientists have produced chemicals to control the spread of disease. These chemicals kill the microbes while they are still outside our bodies in the environment around us.

Chemicals that kill microbes

You can test the effectiveness of these chemicals by adding them to bacteria grown on an agar plate. Look at the two agar plates.

- The same bacterium has been grown on each plate, and they have both been kept in the same conditions.

- One drop of disinfectant was placed in the middle of plate **B**, and no disinfectant was added to plate **A**.

The clear patch in the middle of plate **B** shows that the bacteria in that region have died. They have been killed by the disinfectant.

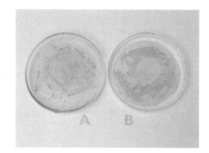

What are antibiotics?

Any chemical which can kill bacteria, fungi or viruses has anti-microbial properties. Antibiotics are medicines which kill only bacteria. Household substances (like the disinfectant used above) can kill bacteria, fungi and viruses, but they work in the surroundings rather than inside our bodies. They are not called antibiotics because they are not medicines.

To get antibiotics from a chemist's shop or pharmacy, you must have a form called a **prescription**. This form must be written out by a doctor. The pharmacist needs the form because he or she needs to know which antibiotic you need. Some antibiotics kill lots of different types of bacteria; some antibiotics kill only one type of bacteria.

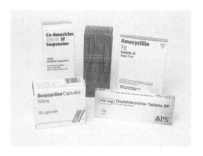

Antibiotics kill only bacteria

You can see how antibiotics affect bacteria by growing different bacteria on agar plates. The type of bacteria that survives and grows depends on which antibiotic is added to the agar.

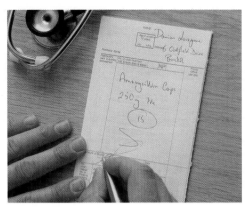

A prescription

Can antibiotics cure diseases caused by viruses?

Chicken pox, flu and the common cold are all caused by viruses. If you are suffering from an illness caused by a virus, there is no point in taking antibiotics. Antibiotics don't destroy viruses, they can only kill bacteria. There are very few medicines available which can destroy viruses. Scientists are trying to increase the number of such medicines by doing research.

What are the problems with antibiotics?

When antibiotics were first discovered, people thought that illnesses would be cured for ever. However, bacteria often become **resistant** to antibiotics. This happens in about one in several million bacteria. Doctors are worried about giving patients antibiotics unless it is really necessary for two reasons:

- If doctors prescribe a general antibiotic which kills all types of bacteria, it will kill off all the normal bacteria, so that the resistant bacteria have more food and more space to live in, and can reproduce more easily.

- When people feel better, they often stop taking their antibiotics before they have finished the full course. It is very important that you finish taking all the antibiotics that the doctor gives you. The more antibiotics you take, the more likely you are to kill off the resistant bacteria.

QUESTIONS

1 Write down the names of two chemicals you could use to kill microbes in your bathroom.

2 You want to test whether a chemical can kill bacteria. Describe an experiment you could do.

3 a What is an antibiotic?

  b Why do pharmacists need a prescription before they can give you antibiotics?

4 Explain why doctors are worried about giving patients antibiotics.

THE HISTORY OF ANTIBIOTICS

TOPIC CHECKLIST

- Who discovered antibiotics?
- What effect have antibiotics had on disease?

Who discovered antibiotics?

The first antibiotic was called **penicillin**. It was discovered by Sir Alexander Fleming. He was growing some *Staphylococci* bacteria on an agar plate. Some *Penicillium* mould also accidentally grew on the plate. In places where the mould was growing, there were no bacteria. The mould made a substance that killed the bacteria. Fleming named the substance penicillin after the mould that produced it.

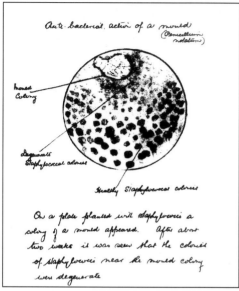

Alexander Fleming's notes

Fleming did not realise at the time that penicillin could be very important in treating disease. Howard Florey and Ernst Chain, from Oxford University, did realise it and in 1940 they found a way of making pure penicillin. On 25th May 1940, they tested it on mice. They injected eight mice with *Streptococcus* bacteria. They also gave four of those mice injections of penicillin. All of those injected with penicillin survived. All of those not given penicillin died. With this evidence, Florey persuaded American drug companies to mass-produce penicillin. By 1944 it was being used on every front line in the Second World War.

What effect have antibiotics had on disease?

Since the war, many more antibiotics have been developed. Rather than produce antibiotics that can kill lots of different bacteria, scientists have developed antibiotics to kill only those bacteria that cause particular diseases. A good example is *Mycobacterium tuberculosis*, which causes the disease tuberculosis.

Tuberculosis is a disease that is spread when people sneeze or cough. If you live or work in crowded conditions, it can spread very easily. It usually affects the lungs by destroying the tissue inside them. It can also affect your white blood cells, stopping you fighting the disease effectively. People with tuberculosis suffer from some fairly unpleasant symptoms including:

- fever
- weight loss
- coughing
- night sweats.

Two antibiotics are used to treat tuberculosis: rifampicin and isoniazid. Patients have to take them for between four and seven months before the bacteria are all killed off. It can take several more months for all traces of the disease to disappear. You can see how important antibiotics have been in treating tuberculosis by looking at the graph below.

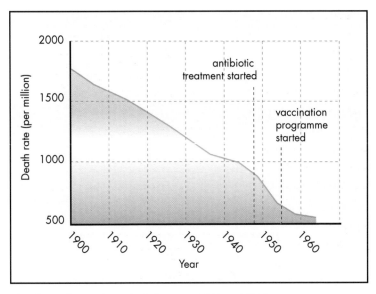

Death rate from tuberculosis between 1900 and 1960

a What effect did antibiotics have on the death rate from tuberculosis?

b Between 1900 and 1940, living and working conditions became less crowded. Explain why this caused tuberculosis to become less common, even though antibiotics had not been introduced then.

c What else mentioned in the graph affected the death rate from tuberculosis?

QUESTIONS

1 Someone has invented a new antibiotic that should kill any bacteria.

a Write down in detail how you would test its effectiveness in a laboratory experiment using agar plates.

b Write down in detail how you would test its effectiveness in a laboratory experiment using real animals.

2 Why was the discovery of penicillin important in helping us to win the Second World War?

PROTECTION AGAINST DISEASE: IMMUNITY AND IMMUNISATION

What is immunity?

When microbes get into your blood, your white blood cells make **antibodies** to kill them. While those antibodies are being made, you may suffer from the disease caused by the microbes. After the antibodies have destroyed the microbes, you get better. Because the antibodies stay in your blood, they are ready to recognise and kill the same type of microbe if it gets into your blood again. This means the microbe has no chance to cause the disease. You have become **immune** (resistant) to that disease.

What is immunisation?

When babies are first born, they have no antibodies in their blood. Any microbes which get into their blood will immediately cause disease. To stop this happening, antibodies are passed from the mother to the baby in her breast milk.

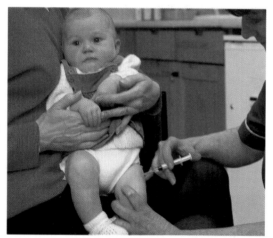

Immunisation is an artificial way of making you immune to a disease. Instead of giving you antibodies, it helps you to make them yourself. You will have been immunised against some diseases when you were younger.

When you are immunised, a **vaccine** is injected into your bloodstream – we say you have been vaccinated, or inoculated with the vaccine.

Vaccines contain the microbes that cause the disease. To stop the vaccine actually giving you the disease, the microbes have been changed slightly:

● they may be dead

● they may have been weakened

● only parts of the microbes are injected.

After the injection, your white blood cells make antibodies against the microbes that were injected in the vaccine.

If the normal, disease-causing microbes enter your blood at a later date, the antibodies are there to recognise and kill them. This means the microbes are killed before they have chance to cause the disease.

Some vaccines do not work very well, and often need boosters. This means giving you a little bit more of the vaccine on a regular basis. The boosters stop the number of antibodies in your blood dropping too low.

a **Why don't vaccinations contain the real, unaltered disease-causing microbe?**

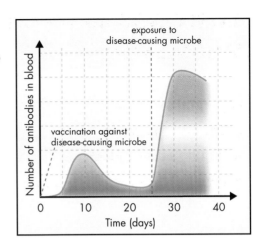

How have vaccinations affected public health?

Immunisation programmes can get rid of diseases completely from the population. Look at the graph. It shows how many children died of diphtheria between 1870 and 1960.

b **How did the use of medicine and the use of vaccinations affect the number of deaths?**

Diphtheria is just one disease for which there is a national immunisation programme. Everyone in this country is immunised against the same diseases when they are children and teenagers. These are called routine immunisations. You may have been immunised against some or all of the diseases in this list:

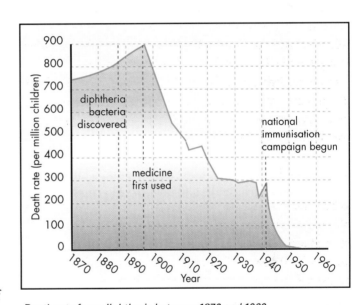

Death rate from diphtheria between 1870 and 1960

- polio
- diphtheria
- whooping cough
- tetanus
- measles
- mumps
- rubella
- influenza
- tuberculosis (TB).

QUESTIONS

1 Explain what happens in your blood if you are infected with a microbe.

2 What is immunisation?

3 How do new-born babies become immune to disease?

4 Name three things a vaccine can contain.

5 The virus that causes colds can change very slightly each year, making it less easy to be recognised. Why does this make it hard to vaccinate against colds?

D Ecological relationships

HOW ARE GREEN PLANTS CLASSIFIED?

TOPIC CHECKLIST

- How do we classify things?
- How do you classify plants?
- How do scientists classify plants?

How do we classify things?

Every living thing has special features (**adaptations**) that help it to survive in its particular habitat. These special features make it look different from every other species. However, even though they are different, species also have features in common. In Unit 7D, you learnt how to put living things into taxonomic groups depending on how many features they have in common. All living things are divided into five groups called kingdoms. In Unit 7D we looked at the animal kingdom. In this unit, we shall look at the **plant kingdom**.

ⓐ Humans and dogs are both in the animal kingdom. Write down two features that humans and dogs have in common.

ⓑ Humans and trees are in different kingdoms. Write down two ways in which humans and trees are different.

How are these leaves different?

How do you classify plants?

Look at the photographs of leaves above. These plants are all very different from each other. They have different adaptations that help them to survive in different habitats. For example, the leaves of mosses and liverworts do not have a shiny waterproof layer (cuticle) on their surfaces. This means they have to live in moist habitats. The other leaf has a shiny cuticle and can live in different habitats.

The plants can be divided into two groups depending on the adaptations they have in common. All plants in one group have two features in common:

- complex leaves with a shiny, waterproof cuticle
- vascular tissue (these are special tubes called xylem and phloem which transport water and food around the plant).

You can divide up the plant kingdom according to any feature you like. For example, one group could contain all the plants that reproduce using seeds, and the other group could contain all the plants that reproduce using spores.

How are these plants different?

You can keep dividing plants into smaller and smaller groups. The plants with seeds can be split into two groups: those with cones and those with flowers. The plants with flowers can be split into two groups: those with seeds containing two cotyledons and those with seeds containing one cotyledon. Cotyledons are seed leaves; they are often used as food stores in the seed. You can see them if you take the skin off a pea or bean and pull the seed apart.

The cotyledons of a pea seed

How do scientists classify plants?

To classify plants into groups, scientists look at all their features. Look at the fact files to see how plants have been divided up. The names in brackets are the Greek names of each group. Botanists (scientists that study plants) often use Greek or Latin names for plants.

Mosses and liverworts (Bryophyta)

thread moss

liverwort

- small
- tiny roots made of one cell
- simple leaves without a waxy cuticle
- no flowers
- reproduce using spores
- live in woodland and other damp, shady places

Conifers (Coniferophyta)

pine tree

pine cone

- very large
- no flowers
- reproduce using seeds
- seeds made inside cones
- live in a variety of habitats; they can live in much drier places than mosses or ferns

Ferns (Filicinophyta)

common fern

bracken

- leaves called fronds are coiled up when in bud
- no flowers
- reproduce using spores
- live in damp places

Flowering plants (Angiospermophyta)

oak tree

grass

rose

- flowers
- reproduce using seeds
- seeds made inside fruits
- found in almost every type of habitat

QUESTIONS

1 Name two plants that may be found in each of these habitats:

a Arctic, **b** English forest, **c** desert.

2 Write down three features you could use to divide plants into groups.

3 Which type of plant can live in the widest variety of habitats?

WHY ARE COMMUNITIES DIFFERENT IN DIFFERENT HABITATS?

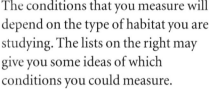

Different environments

What is a community?

Think about the word **community**; you may have a community centre near your home. A community of people includes all the different people who live in a particular place. A community of living things includes all the different species of living things that live in a **habitat**. The community and the habitat together make up the **ecosystem**.

Do environmental conditions affect a community?

To show that **environmental conditions** affect what survives in a habitat, you need to measure the conditions. You can do this by using data-loggers. These are sensors connected directly to a computer. The conditions in a habitat will directly affect which animals and plants can survive there. For example, a frog could not survive in the desert. Its moist skin would dry out too quickly.

The conditions that you measure will depend on the type of habitat you are studying. The lists on the right may give you some ideas of which conditions you could measure.

There are other things that can affect who survives in a particular habitat. You wouldn't live somewhere without any food. Most birds don't live in habitats without any trees.

Water	Soil	Air
temperature	temperature	temperature
water speed	moisture	humidity
amount of dissolved	amount of rotting	light intensity
oxygen	material	wind speed
light intensity	acidity	

a Look at the picture. Explain why birds might choose not to live here. Think about what they need to build in the springtime.

When you measure environmental conditions, you must be aware that one environmental condition may have an effect on another, for example:

- Streams with fast-flowing water may be colder than streams with slow-flowing water.

The Arctic tundra

● Warm conditions and quick growth of plants in ponds can cause oxygen levels to drop.

Once you have measured the environmental factors for a habitat, you can then look at how they affect the community of organisms that lives there. Look at the photographs of the desert and forest habitats below.

ⓑ **Use the table on page 46 to help you to decide what environmental conditions you might measure, so that you could compare the two habitats precisely.**

Case study 1: Desert

Case study 2: Forest

How do organisms adapt to environmental conditions?

Animals and plants have adaptations that help them to survive in a particular habitat. Let's compare living things in streams and ponds.

Water in a stream moves quite quickly. The living things in the stream need adaptations to stop them being swept away or damaged by the fast-flowing water.

A caddis-fly larva

● Freshwater shrimps protect themselves from the current by hiding under stones or between the stems of aquatic plants.

● Caddis-fly larvae build a protective tube and attach themselves to rocks in the stream.

● Trout have strong muscles to help them swim against the flow.

● Plants are rooted into the bed of the stream and have long, flexible stems which stop them being ripped by the fast-flowing water.

Water-weed

The plants and animals in a pond do not need these adaptations because the water moves very slowly.

Normally, the living things in a habitat are adapted to all the environmental conditions there. Each habitat supports many different organisms. Different habitats support a different selection of organisms.

Water-lily on a pond

QUESTIONS

1 What is a community?

2 Choose one of the plants that you have studied. Explain how it is adapted to its habitat.

3 Choose one of the animals that you have studied. Explain how it is adapted to its habitat.

4 Give four reasons why different species survive in different places.

HOW BIG ARE THE POPULATIONS IN A HABITAT?

TOPIC CHECKLIST

- How can you estimate population size?
- What is a quadrat and how do you use it?
- Why do you use a quadrat?

How can you estimate population size?

Imagine you want to find out how many daisies are on the school field (the **population size**). You could go onto the field and count them all. However, this could take you all day and it might be very difficult. When you try to count animals it gets even harder.

Because counting can be so difficult, we use **sampling** to estimate the population size of plants and animals. Imagine a school field that is 10 000 m². You could count how many daisies are in a 1 m² **sample** and multiply that number by 10 000. For example, if you counted four daisies in the 1 m² sample, you would estimate there to be 40 000 daisies in 10 000 m².

(a) **If you counted 10 daisies in a 1 m² sample of a school field that is 10 000 m², how many daisies would you estimate there to be in the whole school field?**

What is a quadrat and how do you use it?

Instead of always having to measure out 1 m², you can use a 1 m² **quadrat**. You throw the quadrat onto the field, and count the daisies inside it when it lands.

A quadrat on a school field

There can be a problem with using quadrats for sampling. Look at the plan of a school field. Each tiny flower symbol is a daisy. If John throws the quadrat near the tree, the quadrat will contain lots of daisies. If he throws the quadrat near the gate, the quadrat will contain very few daisies. If he uses only one of these quadrats to estimate population size, his answer will not be reliable.

To get a realistic estimate of the number of daisies on the field, John must count daisies in more than one quadrat. Instead of

How to throw a quadrat randomly. Be careful!

choosing where to put the quadrats, he must also throw them randomly at different points throughout the field.

ⓑ How many times do you think John should throw the quadrat and count the daisies to get a reliable estimate?

To estimate the population size, he needs to use an equation:

$$\text{population size} = \frac{\text{total number of daisies in all the quadrats}}{\text{number of quadrats}} \times \text{area of field}$$

Sometimes, there are still too many plants (such as grass) to count in 1 m². Instead, you can estimate the percentage of the area in the quadrat that is covered by the grass. For example:

● In the picture, the percentage of the quadrat which is covered by grass is about 75%.

● Estimate the percentage of the area covered in each quadrat.

● Add together all the percentages to get a total percentage for all the quadrats.

● Use an equation to calculate the area of the whole field that is covered by grass:

Using a quadrat to estimate percentage cover

$$\text{area of field covered} = \frac{\text{total of percentages from all the quadrats}}{\text{number of quadrats}} \times \text{area of field}$$

ⓒ Use this equation to work out the area of the field covered by grass in the example below.

Quadrat No.	1	2	3	4	5	6	7	8	9	10
Area covered by grass (%)	20	35	30	10	65	20	15	20	75	30

Why do you use a quadrat?

You can use quadrats to compare the population size of any plant species living in two different areas. If you also measure the environmental conditions in each area, you can work out why different plants live in different places.

ⓓ Which environmental condition affects the number of mice living in each habitat?

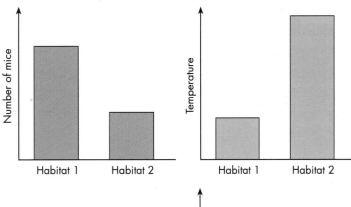

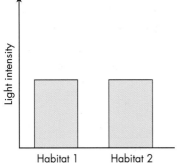

QUESTIONS

1 Why is it difficult to count all the daisies in a field?

2 Why should you throw a quadrat randomly in a field, and not choose where to put it?

3 What is a quadrat used for?

HOW DO THINGS IN A COMMUNITY DEPEND ON EACH OTHER?

What affects population size?

We have already looked at how environmental factors affect what organisms live in a habitat, but these factors can also affect how many of each species can be supported by the habitat. Living things can only survive in particular environmental conditions if they can get the resources they need to survive.

ⓐ **What resources do all living things need to survive?**

In this topic we are going to look at how the other living things in an area can affect how many of each species survives there. In Unit 7C we looked at the relationship between **predators** and **prey**. If an organism has lots of predators, then its numbers may be reduced. We can see how the population of a species may be affected by predation, by looking at the food web for the habitat.

What does a food web show?

A **food web** consists of **food chains** linked together to show the feeding relationships in a community. Food webs always begin with plants. Plants use light energy from the Sun to make chemical energy, which they store as food.

Plants are called **producers** because they *produce* food. The animals in the food web are all **consumers**. The arrows in the food web show the direction in which materials and energy flow through the food web: from the producer to the **primary consumer** to the **secondary consumer**.

ⓑ **What is the name of animals that (i) only eat other animals, (ii) only eat plants, (iii) eat both animals and plants?**

How do populations affect each other?

We can use a food web to work out what would happen if the number of species changed and how it would affect other species' populations. Look at the woodland food web on page 51.

ⓒ **Write out three food chains that you can see in the woodland food web.**

What would happen if someone came into the wood and cut down the oak tree?

- The leaf-eating insects would have no food and die.
- Without the oak tree, the moths would have to eat more of the bushes.

These changes will mean there is less food for the bluetits and the voles; their population size may drop as a result.

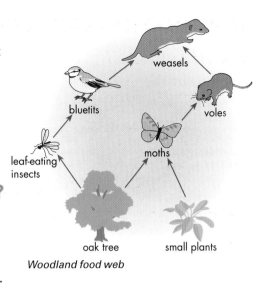

Woodland food web

d What will then happen to the number of weasels?

As you can see, if the population size of one species changes, it can have far-reaching effects throughout the food web.

e The small plants in this food web grow in a clearing in the centre of the wood. The owner of the wood plants three new trees in the clearing. Explain the effect the trees will have on the small plants.

What causes changes in population size?

Environmental conditions can affect population size. A harsh winter or a bad storm could kill off many plants and animals. On the other hand, a mild winter or a good summer could increase the numbers of plants and animals in the population.

Humans can also affect population size. Chemicals may be used on farms to kill weeds, insects and fungi. Some mammals are killed because they are pests. Building roads and houses always involves destroying habitats, leaving the organisms that live there without a home. Pollution from cars and industry poisons rivers and streams. This does not just kill animals and plants that live in the river, it may also poison any animals that drink the water.

Predators can affect population size. A predator is an animal that hunts for and kills another animal for food. The animal it kills is called its prey. Population sizes of predators and prey are said to 'cycle'; this is because they go up and down like the pedals on a bicycle. Look at the graph.

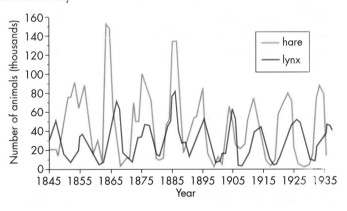

Populations of snowshoe hare and lynx

QUESTIONS

1 How do these organisms get their food?
   a producer
   b primary consumer
   c secondary consumer.

2 Name three things that can affect population size.

3 Look at the African food web. In Africa it only rains during three months of the year. Sometimes the rains fail, and there is no rain for two years! Explain what would happen to the population size of each species if the rains failed.

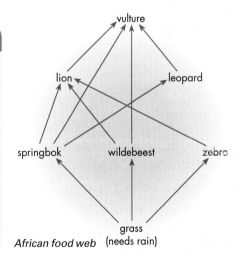

African food web

TOPIC CHECKLIST

- What is a pyramid of numbers?
- How does energy flow through a food chain?
- When is a pyramid not a pyramid?
- How do plants benefit from other organisms in the community?

What is a pyramid of numbers?

Look at this food chain taken from a woodland community. The numbers show the population of each species in the community. You can see that there are more producers than primary consumers, and there are more primary consumers than secondary consumers.

$$\text{grass} \rightarrow \text{insects} \rightarrow \text{blue tits}$$
$$(100) \qquad (20) \qquad (1)$$

Instead of just writing down the numbers, we can use the numbers to draw a bar or box to represent each species and draw them on top of each other to make a pyramid. This is a bit like a bar graph sideways on.

You must remember to draw the boxes to scale. For example, in this food chain 1 mm represents one organism. So the grass box is 100 mm long, the insect box is 20 mm long, and the blue tit box is 1 mm long. It is called a **pyramid of numbers** because it shows the number of each species.

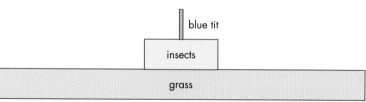

A pyramid of numbers

ⓐ **Draw a pyramid of numbers for this food chain.**

$$\text{dead leaves} \rightarrow \text{worms} \rightarrow \text{blackbird}$$
$$(200) \qquad (4) \qquad (1)$$

How does energy flow through a food chain?

Usually, as you go higher up the pyramid there are fewer organisms. This can be partly explained because organisms higher up the pyramid are often bigger than organisms lower down the pyramid. Look at this food chain:

$$\text{grass} \rightarrow \text{rabbit} \rightarrow \text{lynx}$$

The lynx is bigger than the rabbit and so needs to eat lots of rabbits to stay alive. However, it is important to remember that energy is also lost as it flows along a food chain. Energy enters a food chain through a producer such as grass. The grass stores the energy. The rabbit eats the grass, taking some of the stored energy into its body. But the rabbit runs around and reproduces, both of which use up energy. That means there is less energy available to the lynx who eats the rabbit.

b **Can you think of any other ways in which the rabbit uses up energy?**

When is a pyramid not a pyramid?

Sometimes a pyramid of numbers can be a very odd shape. Look at this food chain and its pyramid of numbers.

oak tree → caterpillar → blue tit
(1)　　　　(60)　　　　(2)

Pyramids like this give a false impression of how energy flows through a food chain. Unless you think carefully about the food chain, it looks like there are not enough producers to feed the caterpillars. In fact, the pyramid is a strange shape because the producer is so large in mass. Lots of caterpillars can feed on one tree because there is so much energy stored within it.

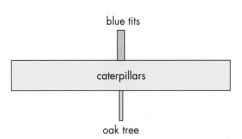

How do plants benefit from other organisms in the community?

In topic D4, we saw how one plant such as a large tree can deprive smaller plants of light, water and nutrients. After all, a tree must absorb a massive amount of nutrients from the soil each year.

All plants make food using energy from the Sun, but to do so, they also need **nutrients**, which they **absorb** from the soil through their **roots**. So how do these nutrients get into the soil and why don't they run out? Look at the picture.

Nutrients are returned to the soil from living things, either through waste (like faeces or urine) or dead material (whole organisms or parts of organisms like dead leaves). This material is often called **detritus**. However, to be absorbed by a plant's roots, the nutrients have to be released from the detritus. This is done by microbes which cause the detritus to **decay** (rot). When this happens, the nutrients are released back into the soil so the plants can use them again. So you see, the tree can reuse the nutrients from its own old leaves, after they have fallen off and been rotted down to release the nutrients into the soil.

QUESTIONS

1 Why are pyramids of numbers normally a pyramid shape?

2 When are pyramids of numbers not a pyramid shape?

3 a How do plants get their nutrients?

　b Why doesn't that supply of nutrients run out?

E Atoms and elements

HOW MANY DIFFERENT MATERIALS ARE THERE?

> **TOPIC CHECKLIST**
> - How many materials are there?
> - What are all materials made from?
> - Some common elements

How many materials are there?

In science, the word 'material' has a particular meaning. It *can* mean the same as in everyday life – a piece of cloth, but scientists use the word 'material' to describe *anything* you can touch – even a gas.

For thousands of years people have been able to distinguish between a large number of materials. For example, it was important to prehistoric people to know the difference between wood and bone, because one burned better than the other.

Ancient people only had natural materials to use, but soon they learned how to change materials to make them more useful. Often this meant that a new material was made. More recently, we have been able to identify what materials are made out of. This has led to us being able to produce completely new materials that cannot be made naturally.

So how many materials are there? No one really knows, except that there are at least several million that we are sure of. People keep inventing more and more, so the number keeps going up.

Different materials

ⓐ **Name one solid, one liquid and one gas from the materials in the photographs above.**

What are all materials made from?

There are millions upon millions of different materials, but all materials are made up from a 'building set' of basic bits that we call **elements**.

Scientists have identified about 100 different elements so far, but there are probably still more to be found. It may seem surprising that millions of different materials can be made from just 100 different elements, but read on and you will understand how it works.

Let's imagine the letters of the alphabet are elements which we put together in different combinations to make new materials. We are not counting combinations with the same letters in different orders.

If we take two letters, A and B, we can make one combination: AB.

If we take three letters, A, B, C, we can make four combinations: AB, AC, BC, ABC.

If we take four letters, A, B, C, D, we can make eleven combinations: AB, AC, AD, BC, BD, CD, ABC, ABD, ACD, BCD, ABCD.

ⓑ **Now write down the combinations you can find for five letters. How many are there?**

By the time you get to 20 'letters or elements' the number of materials that can be made is about a million. So you see we can make a lot of different materials with just a few elements.

Different arrangements of the same atoms can give different materials

Some common elements

You may not realise it, but you already know the names of quite a few of the elements. Some elements do not seem to play a very active part in our lives. But some elements seem to crop up all the time, for example:

hydrogen   *oxygen*   *iron*   *aluminium*   *calcium*
carbon   *copper*   *chlorine*   *magnesium*   *sodium*

The **Periodic Table** shows all the elements we know about.

ⓒ **Find carbon, hydrogen, oxygen and aluminium in the Periodic Table. For each one, write down the letter or letters that go with the name. For example, helium has the letters 'He'.**

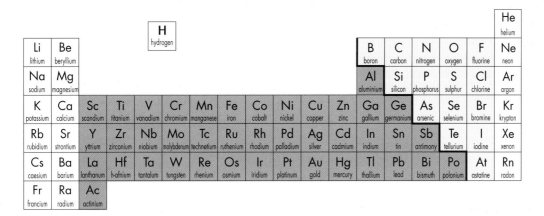

The Periodic Table of the elements

QUESTIONS

1 About how many elements are there?

2 Explain why there are more materials than elements.

3 Write a sentence to explain how an element and a material are different.

What's in an element?

We saw on the last page that there are millions of different materials made up from about 100 different elements. An element can look just like any other material, so let's look at what makes an element an element. We can't see what is inside an element very easily, so we can use a scientific model to help us imagine what it is like.

If you made a scientific model of a lump of an element out of building bricks it could look like the top photograph.

When you take apart the model of an element until it can't be taken apart any more, you are left with a pile of bits that are all exactly the same. In the real element, we call these smallest bits **atoms**. All the atoms must be exactly the same for it to be an element. If they aren't, it isn't an element.

ⓐ For each of the models (A, B and C) in the photograph on the right, write a sentence to explain why it either is or is not an element.

Elements and non-elements

So elements are made from only one kind of atom. Anything that has more than one kind of atom is not an element, so we call it a non-element.

The element hydrogen is made only of hydrogen atoms. We can show this without Lego bricks by drawing the atoms as circles. To show that it is a hydrogen atom, we can mark it with the 'code' or **symbol** for hydrogen, which is 'H'. You can find this symbol on the Periodic Table on page 55. So we could draw a hydrogen atom as:

A model of an element

A pile of atoms

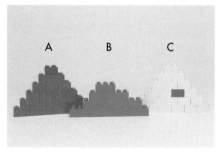
Are these all models of elements?

Notice that the symbol must be a capital 'H' to mean a hydrogen atom.

A little 'h' doesn't mean any kind of atom at all.

The element oxygen is made only of oxygen atoms, so we can draw an oxygen atom in a similar way.

If we draw water in the same way, it looks like this.

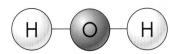

Water is made from both hydrogen and oxygen atoms. There is more than one kind of atom in water, so water is a non-element.

How big are atoms?

We have used the building brick model to talk about elements and atoms because we can see them. Scientists can only see the atoms that make up elements and other materials using the most powerful microscopes. A typical atom might only be one five-millionth of a millimetre across.

Scientists studying chemistry need to think about the way atoms behave and join up to make other materials. To help them do this they often use models as we have done. Another kind of model they use is an atomic modelling kit like the one shown in the photographs below. Each ball represents an atom. It's a bit like our Lego model where each brick represented an atom.

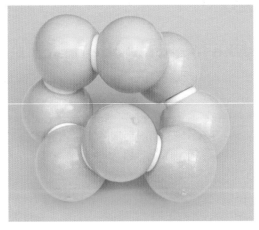

Sulphur

b **Explain whether the photograph of sulphur shows an element or a non-element and why.**

c **Explain whether the photograph of glucose shows an element or a non-element and why.**

Glucose

QUESTIONS

1 What name do scientists use for the *smallest* particles that elements are made of?

2 What is the difference between the particles in an element and the particles in a non-element?

3 How many atoms placed side by side, would fit across one millimetre?

4 Use the Periodic Table on page 55 to find out which elements have these symbols: H, C, N, O, Mg, Al, S, Si, Na, Fe. Write the names and symbols in a table.

WHAT ARE ELEMENTS LIKE?

Who found out about elements?

Today we know a great deal about the elements, but this wasn't always so. Ancient people recognised a few substances that were later found to be elements. Some of the first known elements were gold, silver, copper, iron, carbon and sulphur, although no one called them 'elements' in the way we mean today.

Alchemists and other scientific experimenters discovered many of the elements from the 1600s onwards, but even then scientists had difficulty deciding whether certain substances were elements or not. This problem was not really resolved until the 1800s.

During the last 500 years scientists have put a lot of effort into finding out about the elements. Some scientists didn't want others to read about their discoveries so they wrote them down in code. We now have a vast amount of information that tells us about the elements and how they behave, because modern scientists publish their discoveries so that other people can use them to find out even more.

Old and new information

How do elements differ from each other?

When scientists looked at the elements they had identified, some of the elements looked very different and behaved very differently. However, they also found some looked similar and behaved in a similar way. The way elements look and behave are called **properties**.

The appearance of materials (the way things look) or whether they are solids, liquids or gases are **physical** properties. The way that elements and non-elements alter during chemical changes are **chemical** properties.

Scientists found the best way to make sense of all the information they had about the elements was to classify each element according to its properties.

Elements are different from each other in many ways. They can look different because they are different colours, or because they are shiny or dull. Elements may be solids, liquids or gases at room temperature. They melt and boil at different temperatures, they can be metals or non-metals, and they can be magnetic or non-magnetic.

The properties of an element scientists often look at first are:

- its appearance
- whether it is a solid, liquid or gas at room temperature (20 °C)
- what temperatures it melts and boils at
- whether it is a metal or a non-metal
- whether it is magnetic or non-magnetic.

a **Which of the elements in the photograph are likely to be metals?**

b **Why can't you tell which elements are magnetic?**

How are the elements organised in the Periodic Table?

We have already seen the elements arranged in the Periodic Table. When we colour all the elements that are metals in one colour and all the elements that are non-metals in a different colour, the Periodic Table looks like this:

H																	He
Li	Be											B	C	N	O	F	Ne
Na	Mg											Al	Si	P	S	Cl	Ar
K	Ca	Sc	Ti	V	Cr	Mn	Fe	Co	Ni	Cu	Zn	Ga	Ge	As	Se	Br	Kr
Rb	Sr	Y	Zr	Nb	Mo	Tc	Ru	Rh	Pd	Ag	Cd	In	Sn	Sb	Te	I	Xe
Cs	Ba	La	Hf	Ta	W	Re	Os	Ir	Pt	Au	Hg	Tl	Pb	Bi	Po	At	Rn
Fr	Ra	Ac															

Key
metals non-metals

c **Write one sentence to describe where the metals are in the Periodic Table.**

d **Write one sentence to describe where the non-metals are in the Periodic Table.**

Most of the elements are solids at room temperature. The gases are at the top right of the table.

H																	He
Li	Be											B	C	N	O	F	Ne
Na	Mg											Al	Si	P	S	Cl	Ar
K	Ca	Sc	Ti	V	Cr	Mn	Fe	Co	Ni	Cu	Zn	Ga	Ge	As	Se	Br	Kr
Rb	Sr	Y	Zr	Nb	Mo	Tc	Ru	Rh	Pd	Ag	Cd	In	Sn	Sb	Te	I	Xe
Cs	Ba	La	Hf	Ta	W	Re	Os	Ir	Pt	Au	Hg	Tl	Pb	Bi	Po	At	Rn
Fr	Ra	Ac															

Key
solids liquids gases

e **Write down the names of the gases in the Periodic Table.**

f **Only two elements are liquid at room temperature. What are their names?**

g **Are the two liquid elements metals or non-metals?**

QUESTIONS

1 Write down three ways in which elements can differ from each other.

2 Use a Periodic Table to find out which of these substances are elements: hydrogen, water, sulphur, gold, wood, copper, carbon, air, iron.

3 'Are all metals solids?' Use the Periodic Tables above to answer this question fully.

4 'Are all non-metals solids?' Use the Periodic Tables above to answer this question fully.

HOW DO WE GET ALL THE OTHER MATERIALS?

> ## TOPIC CHECKLIST
>
> - How are non-elements formed?
> - What are compounds?
> - What are molecules?

How are non-elements formed?

When atoms join together with other kinds of atoms the new materials they form are never elements. The new material is often very different from the elements it is made from.

For example, when atoms of carbon, a black solid, join together with oxygen, a colourless gas, they sometimes make carbon monoxide which is a colourless gas. On close inspection, scientists found that in carbon monoxide, one atom of oxygen is joined to one atom of carbon.

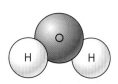

Carbon   +   *Oxygen*   →   *Carbon monoxide*

Water is formed when two atoms of hydrogen react and join together with one atom of oxygen. Both hydrogen and oxygen are colourless gases but the water formed is liquid.

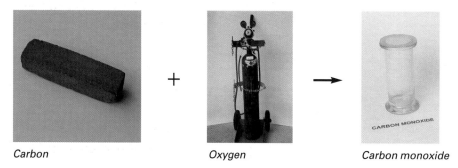

Water is made of two hydrogen atoms joined to one oxygen atom

Carbon monoxide is made of one carbon and one oxygen atom joined together

ⓐ **Write one sentence like those under the diagrams of water and carbon monoxide to describe the arrangement of the atoms in (a) ammonia and (b) methane.**

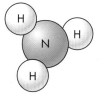

Ammonia

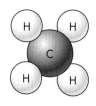

Methane

What are compounds?

A **compound** is a substance that is made of two or more *kinds* of atom *joined* together. Scientists use their atomic modelling kit to show how atoms join together.

Ammonia is a compound because nitrogen and hydrogen atoms are joined together.

Water is a compound because it is made of hydrogen atoms joined to oxygen atoms.

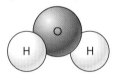

Carbon dioxide is a compound because it is made up of carbon atoms joined to oxygen atoms.

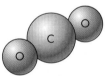

Oxygen is *not* a compound because it only has one kind of atom in it. This means that it is an element.

What are molecules?

A **molecule** is a group of two or more atoms joined together. The atoms can be the same kind or different kinds.

Oxygen is a molecule made of two oxygen atoms joined together. This means that oxygen is a molecule of an element.

Water is a molecule made of two hydrogen atoms joined to oxygen atom. This means that water is a molecule of a compound.

Carbon dioxide is a molecule made of one carbon atom joined to two oxygen atoms.

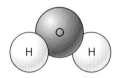

b Is carbon dioxide a molecule of an element or a molecule of a compound?

Helium is not a molecule because its atoms do not join up – they wander round alone.

c Is helium an element or a compound?

QUESTIONS

1 How many kinds of atom are there in a compound?

2 What is the difference between a molecule of a compound and a molecule of an element?

3 Name one element which is a gas and exists as molecules.

4 What is the main difference between a compound and a molecule?

5 A compound is made up of atoms of three different elements. If all three elements are gases, must the compound be a gas too?

HOW CAN WE RECORD THE CHANGES WHEN ATOMS JOIN?

What happens when atoms join?

When atoms of two different elements join together (or combine) to make molecules of a compound, scientists say that a **chemical change** or **chemical reaction** has taken place. If you look at the substances you start off with and the substance you get after the change, they are often very different.

In the picture of a sparkler on the right, atoms of iron are combining with atoms of oxygen to make molecules of a compound called iron oxide. The grey solid iron combines with colourless oxygen gas to make iron oxide which is a black solid.

In the second picture, atoms of copper are combining with atoms of sulphur to make molecules of a compound called copper sulphide. The shiny pink copper combines with yellow sulphur powder to give a black, powdery copper sulphide.

Atoms join as a sparkler burns

Is a new material always made when atoms join?

When two different atoms react together, a chemical change takes place and something new must always be made.

The chemicals that react together are called the **reactants**. The chemicals that are produced are called the **products**.

ⓐ What are the reactants in the photo of the sparkler?

ⓑ What is the product when copper reacts with sulphur?

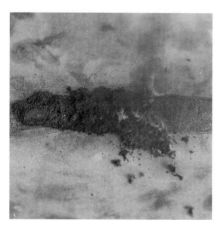

The reaction between copper and sulphur is moving from left to right in this photograph

How can we record these changes?

Over the years, scientists have used many different methods of recording the reactions they observed. Some people couldn't understand other people's methods. Today, there is a way of recording chemical changes that everyone can understand throughout the world. This is a balanced chemical equation and you will learn about these in year 9. For now, there are other ways we can use to record changes to help us understand what is happening. We will look at two different ways.

1 Word equations

Let's look at how to record the reaction between carbon and oxygen to make carbon dioxide. We could write:

carbon *reacts with* oxygen *to make* carbon dioxide.

Instead of writing a sentence, we can use a shorter way of writing the information. This is called a **word equation**. All we do is replace *reacts with* by a '+' sign and replace *to make* by an arrow '→'. Our record of the reaction now looks like this:

carbon + oxygen → carbon dioxide

This is the *word equation* for the reaction between carbon and oxygen.

c Record the following reactions as word equations:

- **hydrogen reacts with oxygen to make water**

- **sodium reacts with chlorine to make sodium chloride**

- **copper reacts with sulphur to make copper sulphide.**

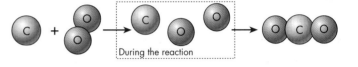

During the reaction

2 Diagrams or models

Another way to record a reaction is to show the individual atoms in a diagram. Every single atom that goes into the reaction, as the reactants, still exists after the reaction in the products. The atoms are just rearranged.

Drawing diagrams is like using the atomic modelling kits that scientists use.

In the diagram above you can see the black carbon and red oxygen atoms. When they react they split apart and then join together again in a new arrangement. Exactly the same thing is shown using an atomic modelling kit in the photographs on the right.

QUESTIONS

1 What is always made when two different kinds of atoms join together?

2 What do scientists call a change like this?

3 If a chemical compound is made, will it be a single atom or a molecule?

4 Write the word equation for magnesium reacting with sulphur to make magnesium sulphide.

5 A metal will react with oxygen to make an oxide. Write word equations for the following metals reacting with oxygen: copper, aluminium, lead.

COMPOUNDS AND MIXTURES

TOPIC CHECKLIST

- Are compounds and mixtures the same?
- Is air a mixture?
- How do we use the substances in air?

Are compounds and mixtures the same?

We already know the difference between elements and compounds. Now we will look at the difference between mixtures and compounds.

Mixtures

- The substances in a mixture are not joined together.

- The substances in a mixture are easily separated. For example, sea water is mainly salt and water. The mixture can be distilled and the water collected.

- Mixtures contain at least two different substances mixed up together. This means that it could be a mixture of elements, or a mixture of compounds, or a mixture of elements or compounds.

- Mixtures have a variable composition: the amount of each substance in the mixture can vary. For example, sea water in the Dead Sea has much more salt in it than sea water in the Atlantic Ocean.

Compounds

- The atoms in a compound are chemically joined together.

- The atoms in a compound are difficult to separate. Once the elements have reacted to make a new compound, you can't easily get the original elements back again.

- Compounds contain atoms from at least two different elements.

- Compounds have a fixed number of atoms of each of the elements. We can show the composition of a compound by its chemical formula, which is always exactly the same for that compound.

ⓐ Draw a table to show the similarities and differences between mixtures and compounds.

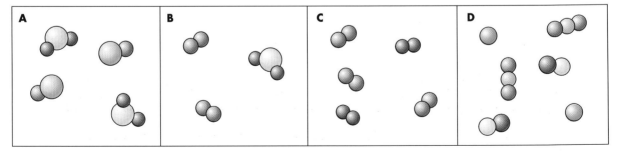

ⓑ Identify what kinds of substance are in each mixture in the diagrams above. For example, one might be a mixture of one element and one compound.

Is air a mixture?

The diagram shows the substances in air.

c **Explain how the diagram shows that air is a mixture.**

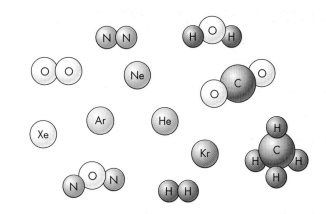

The pie chart shows approximate percentage of each substance, but air is a mixture so the composition of air is not always the same. For example, air near the sea contains more water vapour than the air at the top of a mountain.

The substances in air are not joined together, but are a mixture of gases that can be separated. We often see one of the gases in the air separating from the rest of the mixture. Whenever you see condensation on a cold window you are seeing the water vapour in the air separating from the mixture as tiny droplets of liquid water. We will look at separating the other gases in the mixture on the next page.

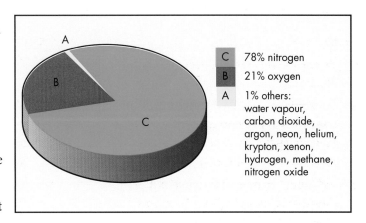

d **Explain why someone's glasses might steam up when coming into a warm room from outside.**

How do we use the substances in air?

Air contains many very useful substances.

- Oxygen is used in making steel, for welding and in breathing apparatus.

- Nitrogen is used for making fertilisers, freezing foods and making electronic components.

- Argon, neon and xenon are widely used in making light bulbs.

- Helium is useful because it is lighter than air so it is good for balloons. It is also mixed with oxygen to make 'artificial air' for divers.

QUESTIONS

1 Write a list of as many mixtures as you can. There are some on this page to start you off.

2 Give at least two pieces of information to explain the difference between *any* compound and *any* mixture.

3 Draw a diagram, like the ones on the previous page, to show a mixture of two elements and two compounds.

MORE DIFFERENCES BETWEEN COMPOUNDS AND MIXTURES

TOPIC CHECKLIST

- Melting points and boiling points of elements and compounds
- Pure substances have fixed boiling and melting points
- Do mixtures have a melting point or a boiling point?
- How do we separate air?

Melting and boiling points

If you heat a solid, it will melt into a liquid. If you cool down the liquid, it will solidify. Both melting and solidifying happen at the same temperature – the **melting point** of a substance.

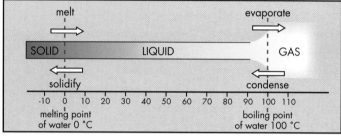

If you heat a liquid, it will evaporate into a gas. If you cool down the gas, it will condense into a liquid. Both evaporation and condensation happen at the same temperature – the **boiling point** of the substance.

Pure substances have fixed boiling points and melting points

In science, 'pure' means 'not mixed with anything else'. Every pure substance – whether an element or a compound – has a fixed melting point and a fixed boiling point. Melting and boiling points are very individual, rather like fingerprints. This means that they can be used to help identify a substance. Two different substances will not have the same melting point and boiling point. One of the two temperatures might be the same, but the other will be different.

0 °C

Pure ice melts at 0 °C

Do mixtures have a fixed melting point or boiling point?

A mixture is made up of two or more substances, so it is impure. A mixture can still melt or boil, but the different substances in the mixture will melt or boil at different temperatures. This means that the mixture will melt across a range of temperatures rather than at one particular temperature. This range of temperatures depends on the amounts of each substance in it.

Pure water freezes at 0 °C and stays at that temperature until all the water has changed to ice. If salt is mixed with the water, the water becomes impure, and no longer solidifies at 0 °C. The mixture solidifies at between – 5 °C and – 20 °C. The melting point is lower because of the salt.

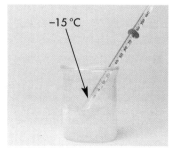

A mixture of ice and salt melts at –15 °C

The same is true for boiling points. Pure water boils at exactly 100 °C, but when some salt is added, the temperature of the boiling mixture rises to between 102 °C and 105 °C. The boiling point of the water has been raised.

Pure water boils at 100 °C

A mixture of water and salt boils at 104 °C

ⓐ Use the information above to explain why salt is put on the roads and pavements in winter.

How do we separate air?

Air is a mixture of different gases, so it can be separated into them. Most of the gases in air boil at such low temperatures that they turn from liquids into gases at temperatures of a couple of hundred degrees *below* zero Celsius. The table below shows these figures.

To separate air into its parts, the air is first **filtered** to remove any tiny particles of soot, dust or **impurities**, then the air is cooled.

ⓑ Look at the table. How far would air need to be cooled so that all the gases in it changed to liquids?

When the substances have **condensed** into liquids, the mixture is gradually warmed. As each substance reaches its boiling point it **evaporates** and becomes a gas which is collected separately.

ⓒ Which gas would evaporate first?

ⓓ Helium changes from a gas to a liquid at −269 °C. What can you say about the state of the other substances in the air at this temperature?

Substance	Melting point (°C)	Boiling point (°C)
nitrogen	−210	−196
oxygen	−218	−183
carbon dioxide	Changes straight from solid to gas	−79
water	0	100
argon	−189	−186
neon	−249	−246
helium	−272	−269

Melting and boiling points of some substances in air

QUESTIONS

1 a What is the melting point of a substance?   **b** What is the boiling point of a substance?

2 Write down the substances in air in the order they would evaporate, lowest boiling point first.

3 At what temperature would all the gases in the air become solids?

4 How could you use information about the melting point and boiling point of a substance to decide whether it was a mixture or a compound?

5 Draw a flow diagram to show the major stages in air separation.

G Rocks and weathering

WHAT ARE ROCKS MADE OF?

> **TOPIC CHECKLIST**
>
> - What is a rock?
> - What are the substances that make up rocks?
> - What are the two main textures of rock?
> - What difference does the texture of a rock make?

slate

What is a rock?

A rock is a solid, naturally occurring, non-living material. Many rocks consist of tiny particles stuck together. To a **geologist** studying the rocks in the Earth's crust, even a material with loose grains can be a rock. This means that materials like clay and sand are rocks, as well as more obviously 'rocky' materials such as slate and sandstone.

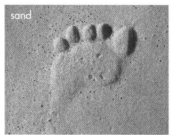
sand

sandstone

What are the substances that make up rocks?

Most rocks are made of a range of different substances called **minerals**. Each mineral is a naturally occurring chemical compound.

To a geologist, even sand is a rock

We can write a chemical formula for each mineral. Different combinations of minerals make different sorts of rocks. Nearly every type of rock is a mixture of different amounts of different minerals.

The minerals in rocks are found as little bits called **grains**. Sometimes the grains can be seen as separate bits with the naked eye, but sometimes you have to use a microscope to be able to see them.

Sometimes every grain in a rock looks exactly the same, and sometimes they look very different from each other. Some grains are **cemented**, or glued, together, and some grains have crystallised to make crystals that all fit perfectly together like a jigsaw puzzle.

ⓐ Do all rocks contain minerals?

ⓑ Do all rocks contain crystals?

ⓒ Why doesn't a rock have a chemical formula?

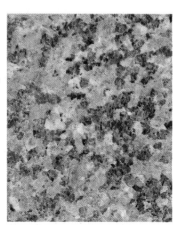
Grains in granite

What are the two main textures of rock?

When we talk about the **texture** of something in everyday life, we usually mean whether the substance feels rough or smooth. The way something feels depends on the way the bits it is made up of fit together.

Rock grains can fit together in two main ways. They may fit together exactly so they leave no spaces between them, giving a texture called an **interlocking** texture. They may fit together leaving tiny spaces between them, giving a texture called a **non-interlocking** texture.

d Which diagram shows an interlocking texture and which shows a non-interlocking texture?

What difference does the texture of a rock make?

We call a rock with a non-interlocking texture a **porous** rock. This means it has spaces between the grains. Some porous rocks can absorb air, oil or water into these spaces. One way of telling if a rock is porous or not is to put it into water. If air bubbles come out of the rock, it must be porous as the air has come out of the tiny gaps between the grains. This cannot usually happen in rocks with an interlocking texture.

e Could oil be found in a rock with an interlocking structure?

f The photograph shows a rock sample in a beaker of water. Does it have an interlocking structure or a porous (non-interlocking) structure?

g If you weighed two rocks with different structures, and then left them in water for a while and weighed them again afterwards, what difference in weight would you expect to see in each rock? Explain your answer.

Porous rocks can hold a lot of air, water or oil, which can have benefits. When it rains, porous rocks can absorb water rather than the water flooding the surface. Oil wells are found where porous rocks trap the oil in the tiny spaces between their mineral grains.

A

rock grain

B
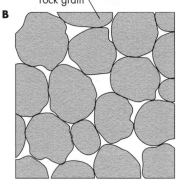

Sandstone

QUESTIONS

1 What does a geologist study?

2 Explain what a rock is and give some examples.

3 Explain what a mineral is.

4 Describe the two main textures of rock.

5 What difference can the texture of a rock make to its properties?

RAIN AND WEATHERING

TOPIC CHECKLIST

- What effects does rain have on rocks?
- How does rain affect rocks?
- What is weathering?

What effects does rain have on rocks?

Rocks get worn away. We can see evidence of this in the weird and fantastic shapes that rocks make – but enjoy them while you can, as the shapes will have changed forever in a few thousand years time. A number of things can cause rocks to wear away, and one of these is rain.

Two gravestones made of the same rock

a **Which rock has been worn away the most by the weather, the one the gravestone is made of or the one the building is made of?**

b **Look at the photographs on the right. For each object, write down as many ways as you can that the rock has changed.**

A partially weathered building

How does rain affect rocks?

Rain causes these effects in different ways. All rainwater is naturally acidic because carbon dioxide from the air dissolves in the rain as it falls, forming a slightly acidic solution. This is not the same as 'acid rain', which is caused by polluting gases dissolving in rainwater to make a much stronger acid.

The minerals that make up the rocks on the right are mica, gypsum and quartz. They are interlocking crystals. Rainwater can slowly dissolve substances such as mica and gypsum, leaving the rock weakened so much that the insoluble parts of it crumble. In this case the quartz is insoluble.

The rain can wear away rocks on the surface of the Earth like these strange outcrops of rock.

The rock in the cave is made of grains of calcium carbonate which are held together by a material called **cement**. It is not the same as the cement we build walls with, nor as strong. The calcium carbonate reacts chemically with the acidic rainwater. The products of this reaction are carbon dioxide which blows away, water which flows away, and calcium oxide which reacts again with the water, making products which are washed away by it. So gradually the rock is weathered, exposing more surface for the water to react with and continue the process.

There is another way rainwater can react chemically with materials in rocks. Some minerals contain substances that react in the presence of water and air to make oxides. In the case of iron-bearing rocks the iron oxide that is made is the same substance you see as rust, so the rock in the photograph on the right really has got rust-streaks on it.

Rain can wear away the rock at natural weaknesses such as cracks to form underground waterways and caves

Rainwater can also change the colour of some rocks. The rust streaks on this rock show where rainwater has reacted with an iron-containing mineral

What is weathering?

Weathering is the word used to describe the ways that rocks are changed. This may be by chemical weathering which makes new substances, or it may be by physical weathering where rock is changed into smaller pieces of the same substance. The two types of weathering can happen together or separately. They are caused by natural processes such as rainfall, wind, waves, sunshine or frost.

QUESTIONS

1 Name one mineral that can be affected by rain.

2 Is weathering a natural process or a man-made problem?

3 Describe what happens during weathering.

4 Explain the difference between chemical and physical weathering.

5 Name two things that water can do to minerals that makes rock wear away.

6 Would a location with high rainfall or one with low rainfall be most likely to suffer fast chemical weathering? Explain your answer.

G3 TEMPERATURE AND WEATHERING

> **TOPIC CHECKLIST**
>
> ● How does temperature affect rocks?
>
> ● What does temperature do to rocks?

How does temperature affect rocks?

The effects of temperature can cause the physical weathering of rocks in two different ways. Both of these processes result in rocks splitting into smaller pieces or fragments due to the forces put on them.

Both photographs show places where the climate produces extremes of temperature which affect the rocks. In the desert, it is very hot by day and very cold at night – almost as low as the freezing point of water. In the mountains, temperatures often fall below the freezing point of water at night but rise above freezing point during the day.

ⓐ In which environment would the daytime temperature be highest?

ⓑ In which environment would the night-time temperature be lowest?

What does temperature do to rocks?

Weathering by heating and cooling

In Unit I we learned that the particles in an object move further apart when they are heated, causing the object to expand. Cooling causes contraction. This happens to the surface of the rock, so it flakes off, or **exfoliates**.

Rocks are mixtures rather than pure substances. This means that each different mineral throughout the rock expands and contracts at a slightly different rate. So some minerals in the rock are expanding and contracting faster than others. This causes stresses to develop in the rock between the grains. As the grains separate slightly due to this force on them, the rock is weakened.

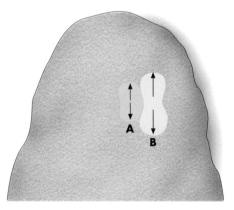

If mineral A expands more than mineral B, a crack may form

In the desert, where the temperature changes by a large amount each day, this cycle of expansion and contraction happens repeatedly. The stresses in the rock make it crack. If a crack is big enough and in the right place, this can cause rock fragments to fall off.

c **If a rock in the northern hemisphere was weathered in this way, which side of the rock would you expect to weather the most?**

'Freeze-thaw' weathering

Rocks often have cracks in them. These may be caused by the stresses from heating and cooling or by movement. If there is a crack in the top of a piece of rock, water can collect in the crack. In mountains where the temperature variation means that the water melts each day and freezes each night, this can cause weathering of the rock.

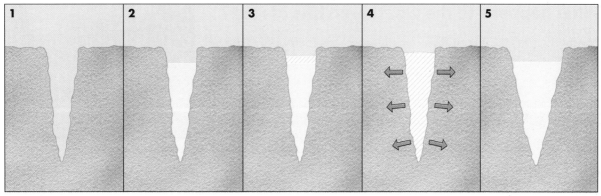

1	2	3	4	5
A crack in a rock . . .	fills with water which . . .	freezes over.	All the water freezes and expands . . .	widening the crack.

As the temperature falls to 0 °C the water will begin to freeze. Water always expands as it turns to ice. It freezes at the top first, which traps water underneath the ice. If the trapped water freezes it tries to expand but has nowhere to expand to, so it pushes against the surrounding rock and ice. This force widens the crack slightly. This process is repeated each time the temperature rises above and then falls below 0 °C. The crack is further widened until the rock splits and a fragment of rock falls off.

QUESTIONS

1 What effect can temperature have on rocks?

2 What are the two ways that temperature can weather rocks?

3 Explain how a change from high to low temperatures can cause weathering.

4 Explain how trapped water can cause weathering.

5 The photograph of Wastwater shows huge piles of fragments broken off by freeze-thaw weathering long ago. What does this tell you about the climate then, in comparison with today?

6 Give two reasons why freeze-thaw weathering is unlikely to happen in a desert.

TOPIC CHECKLIST

- What happens to the weathered bits of rock?
- What is transport?
- What happens during transport?
- Transport and energy
- What is erosion?

Transportation by wind

What happens to the weathered bits of rock?

Weathering isn't the end of the story – it causes fragments of rock to fall onto the ground. They may stay there for a while, but eventually most get moved to somewhere else. Most material is moved by flash floods.

There are a number of ways that rock fragments can be moved. Most of them rely on gravity making things move downhill. Others depend on using energy to overcome gravity and pick up and move fragments.

Transportation by water

What is transport?

Transport is the word scientists use to describe the movement of rock fragments from one place to another. Rock fragments can be transported by:

- being blown by the wind
- being washed along by water
- being carried along by ice.

Transportation by ice

ⓐ Explain how gravity helps to transport a rock fragment being washed down a river.

ⓑ Explain why gravity has to be overcome so a rock fragment can be blown along by the wind.

What happens during transport?

If rock fragments can knock against each other while they are being transported, the corners and sharp edges are worn away so the fragments become rounded and smaller.

A rounded rock fragment has usually been transported. Generally, the smaller and rounder the fragment, the further it has been transported.

Fragments carried by water continually bump into each other

Large, sharp-edged fragments bump together . . .

knocking off corners . . .

and becoming smaller.

and become smaller, rounder pebbles. Grains of sand carried by the wind also bump into each other and become smaller, rounder grains.

Only fragments transported by ice have sharp edges – they don't knock together because when the fragments of rock become embedded in the ice they are held in place.

Weathered rock fragments are broken down further and further until they become pebbles, sand, soil and even clay. All these different sized pieces of broken rock are called **sediments**.

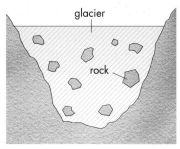

A cross-section of a glacier

Transport and energy

For wind or water to pick up and carry fragments or sediments, the wind or water needs to be travelling fast enough to overcome gravity and pick up the pieces of rock. The larger the fragment, the more energy is needed to move it, so small fragments are moved more easily than large ones. If the wind or water hasn't enough energy, it can't move the sediment.

Wind or water moving quickly has more energy than slow wind or water and so can carry larger fragments. Moving water tends to have a lot more energy than moving air, so water can move larger fragments than air.

Moving water can move fragments by rolling them along the river bed rather than carrying them, but smaller fragments are carried in suspension – they are supported by the moving water pushing against them.

Wind generally carries smaller fragments than water does, but it, too, can roll larger ones along the ground or carry smaller ones suspended.

c Which of the three methods of transport (water, wind or ice) could move the largest sediments?

d Which is likely to be moved further by a river – a small fragment or a large fragment?

What is erosion?

To summarise the last six pages: rocks are *weathered* in a variety of ways, and the fragments of weathered rock are *transported* away by water, wind or ice. Scientists call the combination of these two processes **erosion**. So we can say that: *weathering + transport = erosion*.

QUESTIONS

1 Write down three ways that rock fragments can be transported.

2 Why do fragments transported by rivers have rounded shapes?

3 Why do fragments transported by ice still have sharp edges?

4 Is 'erosion' another name for the weathering of rock? Explain your answer.

WHAT HAPPENS WHEN TRANSPORT STOPS?

Grinding to a halt

When a river slows down – for example when it flows into a lake or into the sea instead of down the side of a mountain – the water no longer has enough energy to move the sediments either by rolling or in suspension. The sediments that can no longer be transported settle to the river or lake bed due to the action of gravity.

The same thing happens to small sediments carried by the wind. As the wind slows down it has less energy to keep particles in suspension, so they fall to the ground. When sediments are put down or deposited, we call the process **deposition**.

ⓐ Which size of sediment stays suspended by the wind for longer, large or small?

Deposition

Sediments can be carried for hundreds or even thousands of miles by fast-flowing water. Rivers can carry large amounts of sediment, and when this sediment falls to the bottom it can quickly build up into a layer or bed. Scientists think that sediments as thick as three centimetres can be deposited in a single day by some rivers such as the Yellow River in China. Most deposits in lakes or seashores are washed away by currents and tides as quickly as they are formed, but sediments remain where they are, when deposited on the seabed.

Yellow River

Sediments are not all dropped at once – the largest fragments are dropped first and the smallest last. In a powerful flow of water the sediments can be carried hundreds of miles out to sea before the water slows down enough, so that the finer sediments can no longer be carried. Some locations will have more deposits of one size of sediment than others.

ⓑ Look at the photograph of the Yellow River. What causes the colour of the water?

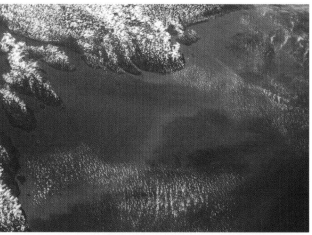
Satellite photo of the Amazon River flowing into the Atlantic

What is deposited where?

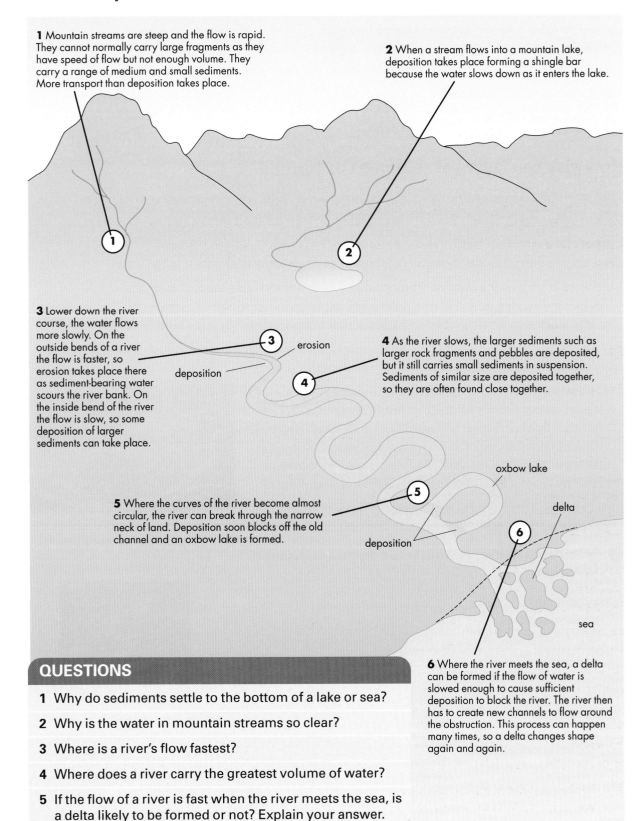

1 Mountain streams are steep and the flow is rapid. They cannot normally carry large fragments as they have speed of flow but not enough volume. They carry a range of medium and small sediments. More transport than deposition takes place.

2 When a stream flows into a mountain lake, deposition takes place forming a shingle bar because the water slows down as it enters the lake.

3 Lower down the river course, the water flows more slowly. On the outside bends of a river the flow is faster, so erosion takes place there as sediment-bearing water scours the river bank. On the inside bend of the river the flow is slow, so some deposition of larger sediments can take place.

erosion

deposition

4 As the river slows, the larger sediments such as larger rock fragments and pebbles are deposited, but it still carries small sediments in suspension. Sediments of similar size are deposited together, so they are often found close together.

oxbow lake

delta

5 Where the curves of the river become almost circular, the river can break through the narrow neck of land. Deposition soon blocks off the old channel and an oxbow lake is formed.

deposition

sea

6 Where the river meets the sea, a delta can be formed if the flow of water is slowed enough to cause sufficient deposition to block the river. The river then has to create new channels to flow around the obstruction. This process can happen many times, so a delta changes shape again and again.

QUESTIONS

1 Why do sediments settle to the bottom of a lake or sea?

2 Why is the water in mountain streams so clear?

3 Where is a river's flow fastest?

4 Where does a river carry the greatest volume of water?

5 If the flow of a river is fast when the river meets the sea, is a delta likely to be formed or not? Explain your answer.

How else can layers of sediment be formed?

Sediments being deposited by wind or water slowing down is one way of forming a layer or bed of sediment. Sediments can also be formed by **evaporation** or **accumulation**.

Evaporation

There are two different ways in which evaporation can cause layers of sediment to build up.

1   If water is trapped in a location where none can be added and none can flow away, the water evaporates, leaving behind a layer of the substances which were dissolved in the water. This gradually turns into a rock which is called an evaporite rock because of the way it has been formed.

Five million years ago, the whole of the Mediterranean Sea evaporated and then filled up again about 40 times in succession, leaving evaporite rock about 2 km thick.

2   This is when the Sun warms a shallow, sub-tropical sea or a coral lagoon. Some of the water at the surface evaporates, and minerals that had been dissolved settle to the sea bed. However, the water that has evaporated is replaced by water flowing into the sea or lagoon, so the water level stays the same. Sediments build up over millions of years, making thick layers.

Parts of Britain are on a bed of rock formed in this way millions of years ago when the climate was very warm and tropical.

A great place to go and study rock formation – if you can stay long enough!

ⓐ **Where in the photograph will the new deposits of sediment be formed?**

Accumulation

When microscopic sea creatures die, their bodies usually rot away and their shells or bones stay on the seabed. Over a period of thousands of years, a considerable layer of 'shelly' material can **accumulate** (build up) on the sea bed. The shells are **compacted** (crushed together) by the

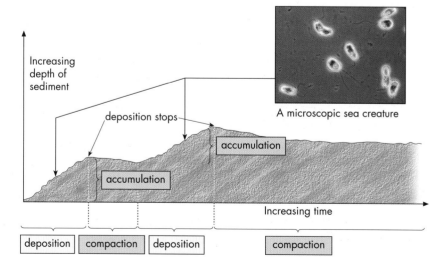

A microscopic sea creature

weight of material piling up on top of them. They can be **cemented** together by minerals such as calcite from the water trapped between the grains.

Burial and bedding planes

Once the water has deposited its load of sediment in layers, the sediment is covered by more sediment, either of the same kind or a different kind. This process is called **burial**. Burial causes the lower sediments to be squashed under the immense pressure of the sediments above.

Each layer in a sedimentary rock is called a **bed**. Each layer is different depending on what it is made from. A thick bed shows that a larger amount of material has been deposited than in a thin bed. However, beds that have been buried deeper will tend to be compacted more than beds near the surface. The line where beds meet is called a **bedding plane**. Sharp bedding planes are formed when there is a time-gap between the deposition of the different layers.

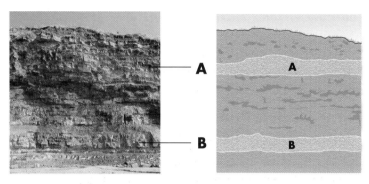

ⓑ Which bed, A or B, will be more compacted? Explain your answer.

A historical record?

Deposition, evaporation and accumulation can form many layers of sediment in a single place. Over millions of years, **compaction** and **cementation** change the layers from loosely packed sediments to rock. The photograph shows layers or beds of rock in a coastal cliff.

ⓒ Which bed, A or B, must have been deposited first? Explain your answer.

Fossils can be found in rocks. Fossils are often either the imprint or cast of where a dead animal or plant was squashed inside deposited sediments, or they can be the hard parts of the organism which have been preserved while the soft parts have rotted away. If a geologist found a fossil at 'A' and another fossil at 'B' in the beds shown above, she would know that fossil 'B' was older than fossil 'A'. If two fossils of the same kind, such as ammonites, are found in different places on Earth, this means that the rocks they are in are probably about the same age, so fossils can help geologists date rocks.

QUESTIONS

1 What is the difference between a 'bed' and a 'bedding plane'?

2 What will happen to the thickness of a bed of sediment when it is compacted and why?

3 Why can we find preserved shells and bones as fossils, but not the soft parts of organisms?

4 Write a few sentences to explain why we find older fossils further under the ground than younger fossils.

H The rock cycle

MAKING SEDIMENTARY ROCKS

TOPIC CHECKLIST

- How are sedimentary rocks formed?
- What do sedimentary rocks look like?
- Examples of sedimentary rocks

How are sedimentary rocks formed?

In Unit G we saw that sediments could form layers or **beds** of material. Now we will look at how layers of sediment change into new rock. The process of rock formation takes millions of years and requires incredible amounts of energy. A bed of sediment may be squashed by being buried under more and more layers of sediment. Alternatively, a bed of sediment may be squashed by earth movements. This process is called **compaction**. Compaction puts the sediments under pressure.

Under pressure, any water in the sediment is heated by the squashing process and then very slowly squeezed out. Minerals such as silica and calcite that had been dissolved in the water stay in the spaces between the grains of sediment, and act as glue to hold the grains together. The process of gluing the grains together is called **cementation**. The result is that sediments are turned into **sedimentary rocks**.

Pebbles – a sediment

Conglomerate – the rock formed from the pebbles

a **What can you see in the photographs that tells you that pebbles are a sediment and conglomerate is a rock?**

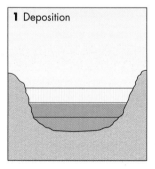

1 Deposition

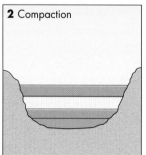

2 Compaction

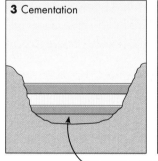

3 Cementation

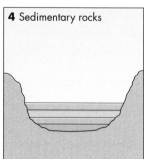

4 Sedimentary rocks

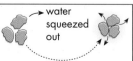
water squeezed out

What do sedimentary rocks look like?

It is useful to know the important features of sedimentary rocks so that you can easily recognise one when you see it. These **characteristics** are easy to see in some sedimentary rocks and almost invisible in others. The more of these features you identify in a rock, the more certain you can be that the rock you are looking at is a sedimentary rock.

Sedimentary rocks:

- have **grains**, not crystals, which are held together by **cement**
- are often **porous** because most have air spaces between their grains
- mostly have a non-interlocking texture
- can contain **fossils**.

Examples of sedimentary rocks

Here are a few examples of the many types of sedimentary rocks which exist.

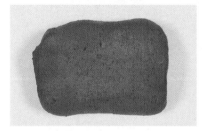

Clay is formed from fine mud. Clay isn't as hard as many rocks, particularly when wet

Limestone is made of calcium carbonate grains, often from bits of shells. The fossil is an ammonite that was covered by the sediment.

This fragment looks like a sedimentary rock, but it isn't. It's a bit of house brick. It is not always easy to identify rocks just by looking.

Sandstone is made of tiny, insoluble quartz grains cemented together

Chalk is another rock made of very fine grains of calcium carbonate

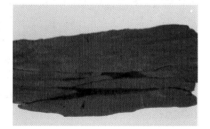

Shale is another sedimentary rock formed from fine compressed mud

b **Name two rocks that contain the mineral calcium carbonate.**

c **Which rocks can be formed from mud?**

QUESTIONS

1 Name the main stages in the formation of a sedimentary rock.

2 Make up a **mnemonic** to remember the characteristics of sedimentary rocks.

3 Explain what 'cementation' is.

4 Using information from the photographs above, explain why it is possible to confuse a piece of house brick with a sedimentary rock.

5 Design a key to identify the sedimentary rocks shown on this page, using the main characteristics of sedimentary rocks and information from the photos.

ARE ALL LIMESTONES THE SAME?

TOPIC CHECKLIST

- What is limestone made of?
- Different kinds of limestone
- How much carbonate is there in limestone?

What is limestone made of?

Limestone is just one type of sedimentary rock but it can be formed in a variety of ways, so it is not surprising that there are many different kinds of limestone. If you pick up two pieces of rock labelled 'limestone' they could be very different, chemically. This is because limestone is made from a mixture of grains of different minerals cemented together, so the composition of limestones can vary. When there are different amounts of each mineral in the mixture, this can make the colour of the limestone vary too.

Many of the minerals in limestones are carbonates, and usually at least 50% of the carbonates are calcium carbonate. The chemical composition depends on what the grains of minerals are and what they are cemented together with. This in turn depends on the way they were formed.

Different types of limestone

Different kinds of limestone

Some limestones were formed in the hot lagoons of coral reefs. Some were formed in shallow, sub-tropical seas where evaporation led to the formation of a white 'lime' mud that settled to the bottom of the sea and built up over millions of years. The photographs here show limestones which have been made in different ways.

Chalk contains the same mineral, calcite, that is in many other limestones. In chalk, the calcite didn't fully harden.

Chalk and a crystal of the mineral, calcite

Travertine is a form of limestone that is often found in caves. This is the limestone that can produce stalagmites and stalactites.

Stalactites and stalagmites in a cave

Tufa in Mother Shipton's cave

A form of limestone called tufa can form from the evaporation of some spring waters.

Coquina

One type of limestone, called coquina, is formed from shells and coral.

Oolitic limestone

Oolitic limestone was formed by calcium carbonate deposits building up on grains of sand that were rolled across the sea floor by wave action.

How much carbonate is there in limestone?

In Year 7 we saw that carbonates react with acid. This gives us a useful test for limestone. First, the rocks are crushed to a powder. Then hydrochloric acid is added to the powder. The mixture fizzes due to carbon dioxide being released as the acid reacts with the carbonate part of calcium carbonate in the limestone. This is the word equation for the reaction:

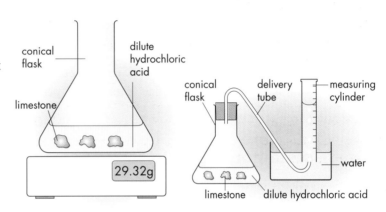
Two ways of measuring the CO_2 produced

hydrochloric acid + calcium carbonate → calcium chloride + carbon dioxide + water

This test doesn't absolutely prove that the rock is limestone, but is one piece of evidence that the rock contains a carbonate. The more carbonate there is in the rock, the more gas will be produced. We can collect the gas produced to measure how much there is.

QUESTIONS

1 How was most limestone formed?

2 What type of limestone is often found in caves?

3 What is coquina formed from?

4 Describe how to measure the amount of carbonate in a rock.

5 Using your knowledge of the properties of mixtures, explain why different mixtures of minerals will give different types of limestones.

METAMORPHIC ROCKS

TOPIC CHECKLIST

- What is a metamorphic rock?
- How are metamorphic rocks formed?
- What are metamorphic rocks made from?

What is a metamorphic rock?

Metamorphic rocks are made from sedimentary rocks that have been changed by heat or by both heat and pressure. When rocks change like this, scientists say the rock has *metamorphosed*, which is where the name comes from.

The main characteristics of metamorphic rocks are that they have crystals in them and that the crystals are usually arranged in layers or bands. The crystals are often too small to see with the naked eye. The crystals usually fit together very closely, so metamorphic rocks tend to have an interlocking structure. Metamorphic rocks don't have fossils in them, because the fossils are deformed or destroyed when the rock changes. Other characteristics of metamorphic rocks will depend on which sedimentary rocks they were formed from.

ⓐ **Explain why metamorphic rocks don't have fossils in them.**

How are metamorphic rocks formed?

Metamorphic rocks can be formed when sedimentary rocks are heated over millions of years. The heat can come from the rocks being squashed, by earth movements, or by the rocks moving so deep in the crust that they are warmed by the hot magma in the mantle or near a volcano.

During metamorphism, the separate grains of the rock stay solid but change into crystals of new minerals. If the rock is under pressure these crystals slowly reorganise into a more regular arrangement – because the pressure makes them line up. This is why metamorphic rocks often have bands or layers in them.

Some metamorphic rocks, like marble, are formed due to heat, and others, like slate, are formed due to pressure *and* heat.

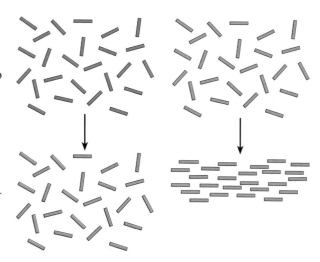

Heat or pressure can make the minerals in the rock change into new minerals

When the rock is squeezed, the particles tend to line up in layers

ⓑ **Give two ways in which metamorphic rocks are different from the rocks they are made from.**

What are metamorphic rocks made from?

There are lots of different metamorphic rocks. We have already looked at one reason for this which depends on *how much* heat and pressure are involved in the change. In the photographs below you can see that another factor is the type of sedimentary rock which is metamorphosed.

Here are some examples of metamorphic rocks and their original sedimentary rocks.

When limestone is heated, the grains of calcium carbonate re-crystallise to give a bright, white colour, while any impurities gather into thin, coloured veins through the rock.

When sandstone is metamorphosed by heat or by pressure, the quartz grains make larger, harder crystals in the rock, metaquartzite.

When shale is heated it makes a rock known as hornfels. When shale is heated *and* put under pressure, it changes into slate instead. If slate is heated and squashed even more, it metamorphoses again into schist, and if the pressure and temperature are really high the schist can change yet again to form gneiss.

Limestone

Marble

Sandstone

Metaquartzite

Shale

heat

Hornfels

heat and pressure

Slate

high temperature and pressure

Schist

very high temperature and pressure

Gneiss

The formation of hornfels, slate, schist and gneiss from shale

QUESTIONS

1 Describe the main characteristics of metamorphic rocks.

2 What metamorphic rock is formed from limestone?

3 Name one metamorphic rock that is formed from shale.

4 What two factors can cause rocks to metamorphose?

5 Describe what happens to the crystals in a rock during metamorphism.

TOPIC CHECKLIST

- How are igneous rocks formed?
- How do crystals form in different rocks?
- How fast is fast?
- What do igneous rocks look like?

This igneous rock was formed deep underground and was slowly uplifted to the surface

How are igneous rocks formed?

Igneous rocks are *always* formed from other rocks which have melted and then cooled down and solidified. Melted or molten rock is called **magma**. It forms under the surface of the Earth's crust. Magma is **viscous**, which means that it *is* a liquid and can flow, but is thick and sticky.

Igneous rocks almost always have crystals in them, which form during the cooling. Magma cools and solidifies into rock in two ways. The first way involves magma cooling underground. The rock above is weathered and removed, exposing the igneous rock. The second way involves molten magma rising from under the crust to the surface through a crack and then cooling on the surface of the Earth.

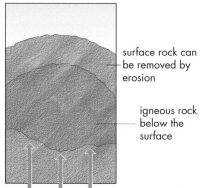

surface rock can be removed by erosion

igneous rock below the surface

forces caused by earth movements push igneous rock upwards – **uplifting**

How do crystals form in different rocks?

Nearly all igneous rocks are made up of crystals of minerals. The size of the crystals varies in different types of igneous rocks. It can vary from hundredths of a millimetre to a few centimetres, but occasionally crystals can grow to more than a metre long.

Gabbro

Granite

Pumice

Basalt

The size of the crystal depends on how long the rock takes to cool down. If the rock cools down quickly, the crystals do not have time to 'grow', so they are small. If the rock cools down slowly, particles in the molten rock have time to clump together to form large crystals.

Igneous rocks which form underground cool very slowly, so they tend to contain large crystals. Igneous rocks which cool on the surface of the Earth cool faster and so contain smaller crystals.

a Which of the rocks in the photographs on page 94 have large crystals?

b Which of the rocks in the photographs cooled down quickly?

c Which of the rocks in the photographs were formed underground?

d Which of the rocks in the photographs were formed on the surface?

How fast is fast?

We are used to talking about rock formation in terms of millions of years, but rapid cooling of molten igneous rock can take a very short time. When lava flows into the sea and is cooled by sea water it can solidify in minutes, although it stays hot for a considerable length of time. When lava is cooled on the Earth's surface by air it takes longer, up to several weeks. Slow cooling underground, on the other hand, occurs over hundreds or thousands of years.

What do igneous rocks look like?

Different igneous rocks have different appearances. This is partly caused by the size of the crystals they are made up of, and partly by the minerals that are in them.

Basalt is an igneous rock made of dark-coloured minerals, such as iron-rich minerals, which colour the rock. Some granites are made of three very different minerals – feldspar which is pink or white, quartz which is grey, and black mica. This gives the granite a 'spotty' appearance.

Igneous rocks are formed from melted rock, so they don't contain fossils because the fossils are made of rock and they melt with the rest of the rock around them and are destroyed as in metamorphic rocks. There is more about the other properties of igneous rocks over the page.

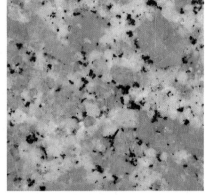

Granite

Basalt

QUESTIONS

1 What have all igneous rocks got in common, apart from crystals?

2 Name two igneous rocks with large crystals.

3 Name two igneous rocks with small crystals.

4 Are igneous rocks likely to be porous?

5 Why are the crystals in some igneous rocks larger than in others?

HOW CAN WE COMPARE IGNEOUS ROCKS?

The hardness of minerals

So far we have compared the appearances of igneous rocks by looking at their colour or crystal size. We can also compare other characteristics, such as their hardness and their density. Both these characteristics depend on the minerals in the igneous rocks.

The hardness of minerals is measured against **Mohs' scale**. This is a scale of one to ten, where one is the very soft rock called talc, and ten is diamond, the hardest known mineral.

a Which is the hardest mineral in the table on the right?

b Which mineral is softer than calcite?

Mineral	Mohs' hardness scale
Black mica	2
Quartz	7
Pyroxine	6
Calcite	3
Olivine	6.5
Feldspar	6

How can we work out the density of a rock?

The density of a rock varies according to the different minerals in it, because some minerals are more dense that others. If we want to decide whether a rock is 'heavier' or a 'lighter' than another rock, we must make sure the comparison is fair. If one rock is bigger than the other rock then the bigger one may have more mass even if it is made of a 'lighter' rock. To get around this problem we could compare the masses of blocks of identical size, but this means cutting pieces of rock into identical sized blocks which is hard to do.

Instead, we measure the mass and volume of any two different pieces of rock and work out the density of each. To measure the mass of each piece of rock we weigh it to find the mass in grams. As we learnt in year 7, when you put an object in water it will displace exactly the same volume of water. This means that we can use the eureka beaker to measure the volume of a rock in cm^3.

Then we use the following equation to calculate the density.

$$density = \frac{mass\ of\ rock\ (in\ g)}{volume\ of\ rock\ (in\ cm^3)}$$

Density is measured in grams per cubic centimetre or g/cm^3.

This block of marble has a mass of 2800 g, and a volume of 1000 cm^3. We can calculate its density like this:

density = mass/volume

   = 2800 g/1000 cm^3

   = 2.8 g/cm^3

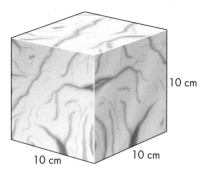

10 cm

10 cm   10 cm

Why are 'heavy' rocks heavy?

If some rocks are more dense than others, it must be because of what is in the rock – what the rock is made of. Igneous rocks tend to be rich either in iron minerals or in silica minerals.

Iron is denser than silica, so iron-rich igneous rocks are usually more dense than silica-rich igneous rocks.

The table below gives information about the mass and the volume of three rock samples.

Name	Mass	Volume
Gabbro	302 g	100 cm^3
Granite	552 g	200 cm^3
Peridotite	987 g	300 cm^3

c Calculate the density of each rock in the table above.

d Gabbro is an iron-rich rock. Does this agree with your density calculations?

e Is peridotite likely to be iron-rich or silica-rich? Explain your answer.

QUESTIONS

1 Write down three characteristics that we could use to compare different igneous rocks.

2 Why might one igneous rock be denser than another igneous rock?

3 What is the density of a sample of rock whose volume is 50 cm^3 and whose mass is 151 g?

4 Use the data table to work out which rock the sample in question 3 is likely to be.

What is the rock cycle?

We already know that:
- igneous rocks are formed from rocks that have been melted
- sedimentary rocks are formed from the weathered remains of other rocks
- metamorphic rocks are formed from sedimentary rocks that have been squashed and heated.

The **rock cycle** is a way of linking together all these natural processes by which rocks are formed and changed. It shows how rocks on the Earth are continuously, though slowly, transformed from one type to the next.

It's all one big system

We can draw a simple diagram to represent the rock cycle. The diagram here shows this. But the real picture has become rather more complicated as scientists have learnt more and more about how our world is shaped by natural forces and processes.

We can see that all rock is recycled from other rock, and that means *all* the rock that makes up our planet. These processes tend to take hundreds of millions of years, so when you look at rocks you don't 'see' the rock cycle in action, just snapshots of small parts of the cycle. It is quite easy for us to understand the formation of igneous rocks at the surface by the cooling of lava from volcanoes because we can see it happening. We can also find clear evidence for the gradual weathering and transport of sediments to form deposits that will eventually turn into sedimentary rocks.

It is harder to appreciate the processes that happen underground. We can't see how deposited sediments change into rock, and how this rock can change or metamorphose into new types of metamorphic rock. It is thought that the temperature in the centre of our planet may be as high as 6000 °C. This heat melts rocks under the crust, which is 6400 km away

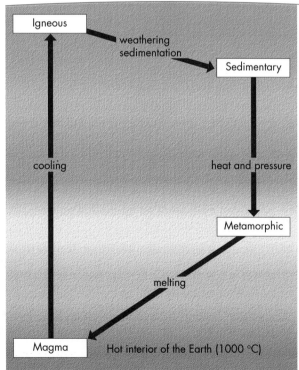

Cool surface of the Earth (10 °C)

Igneous → weathering sedimentation → Sedimentary

cooling

heat and pressure

Metamorphic

melting

Magma — Hot interior of the Earth (1000 °C)

from the centre of the Earth. Under the crust the temperature isn't as high – a mere 1000 °C. When the hot, sticky, flowing magma escapes through cracks in the crust to cool on the ground we call it **lava**.

The rock cycle

The diagram shows a section of the Earth and where all the processes you have learned about happen in order to recycle rocks.

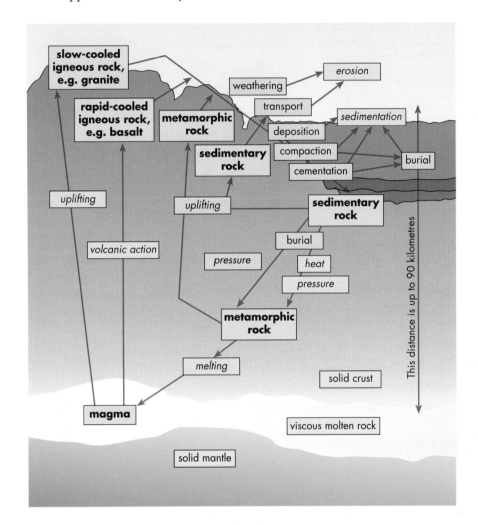

QUESTIONS

1 What type of rock is made from sedimentary rock by **a** melting, **b** heat and pressure?

2 What type of rock is made from metamorphic rock by **a** weathering, **b** melting?

3 What type of rock is made from magma by cooling?

4 Draw your own simple flow diagram to show the most important features of the rock cycle. Use the information in the rock cycle diagram above.

5 Describe what *might* happen to a grain of sand on a beach over millions of years.

I Heating and cooling

WHAT'S THE TEMPERATURE?

TOPIC CHECKLIST

- How hot does it feel?
- How do we measure temperature?
- Measuring extremes of temperature
- How does a thermometer work?

ahh . . . hot!!

that's so cool!!

10 °C

How hot does it feel?

How hot or cold something is, is called its **temperature**. Our bodies can sense how warm or cold materials are, but as measuring devices our senses are not very good. We cannot sense small differences in temperature, and how hot something feels depends on how hot or cold we are.

If your hand is very cold and you put it into slightly warm water, it feels very hot. The same water can feel cold to someone with a hot hand. If your feet are cold when you first get into a bath, it can feel almost too hot to keep your feet in, but as you warm up, the water seems to feel cooler.

Your sense of temperature works by comparing your own temperature with the temperature of the material you touch. We need a better way to measure and compare temperatures that everyone can use.

How do we measure temperature?

Thermometers are devices used to measure how hot things are. The word thermometer is made up of two parts, *thermo* – to do with heat, and *meter* – to do with measuring. The unit generally used to measure temperature is **degrees Celsius**. This is written °C.

On this scale, our own body temperature is normally 37 °C. Ice melts at 0 °C and water boils at 100 °C. Temperatures lower than 0 °C are negative. Temperatures in Britain may drop to −10 °C or even lower when it is frosty in winter.

ⓐ Why do you think that the freezing point and boiling point of water are used as fixed temperatures in arranging the Celsius temperature scale?

You may have heard of other temperature scales. The kelvin scale goes from the coldest possible temperature of −273 °C but calls it 0 K. So ice melts at 273 K and water boils at 373 K.

Measuring extremes of temperature

Our bodies keep themselves almost constantly at 37 °C. Our temperature usually varies only by very small amounts, even when we have a fever. This means we need a thermometer to take our temperature which is very accurate over a small range.

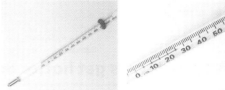

Clinical thermometer

ⓑ Why would a 0 °C to 100 °C thermometer be useless to a doctor examining a patient?

If you want to make toffee or fudge by boiling sugar you will need a thermometer which is less accurate but has a bigger range, up to 250 °C, because sugar boils at a higher temperature than water.

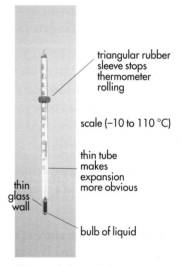

Stirring rod thermometer

Measuring other extremes of temperature, like those found out in space, needs special thermometers. The temperature of the Sun's solar corona is 1 000 000 °C. The temperature at the surface of Pluto is −230 °C.

How does a thermometer work?

The most common type of thermometer is like the stirring rod thermometer you use in the science lab. It contains either mercury which is a silver colour, or alcohol which is usually dyed. It has a bulb of liquid at the bottom end, with a very thin tube leading up the length of the thermometer.

As the liquid inside the thermometer gets warmer it expands. The liquid is contained in a thin tube so that when it expands, its movement up the tube is more noticeable. The temperature is read by seeing how far the liquid moves up the tube. As the liquid gets cooler it contracts and moves back down the tube.

Mercury thermometers are more accurate than alcohol ones, but more expensive. It can be dangerous if a mercury thermometer gets broken because mercury is poisonous.

triangular rubber sleeve stops thermometer rolling

scale (−10 to 110 °C)

thin tube makes expansion more obvious

thin glass wall

bulb of liquid

How a stirring rod thermometer works

QUESTIONS

1 The tube leading up from the bulb in a thermometer is very thin. Explain why.

2 Why do many teachers prefer to use alcohol thermometers rather than mercury ones?

3 A liquid that boils above 100 °C is used inside a stirring rod thermometer. Explain why.

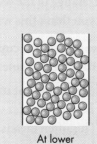

At lower temperatures the particles vibrate less so take up less room

At higher temperatures the particles vibrate more so take up more room

TEMPERATURE AND HEAT ENERGY

How are temperature and heat energy different?

Two things can have the same temperature but contain different amounts of heat energy. Let's look at two examples to explain this.

1 Two beakers of water at 50 °C are at the same temperature, but if one is twice as big as the other, it will contain twice as much heat energy (A and B).

2 A beaker with hot liquid in it will contain more heat energy than one with cooler liquid of the same volume (A and C, or B and D).

We can think of temperature as the *average* amount of energy per particle. Remember in topic I2 we said that particles in the same material can have slightly different amounts of energy. Heat energy is the *total* amount of energy of all the particles in the material.

What happens when we mix hot and cold?

If we mix together two beakers with the same mass of water but at different temperatures, the temperature of the mixture will be an average of the two temperatures. For example, if 200 g of water at 10 °C and 200 g of water at 20 °C are mixed, the result is 400 g of water at 15 °C.

Because the two masses of water are equal, they have an equal effect on each other's temperature. The temperature of the mixture will be the average of the two temperatures.

$$\text{average temperature} = \frac{10 + 20}{2} = \frac{30}{2} = 15\,°C$$

a What would be the temperature of a mixture of two equal masses of water, one at 80 °C and the other at 30 °C?

b How would the temperature of the mixture be affected if there was a larger mass of cooler water?

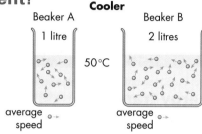

Cooler

Beaker A — 1 litre   50 °C   Beaker B — 2 litres

average speed   average speed

The liquids in these two beakers are the same temperature, so the particles have the same average speed

To heat both liquids by the same amount, the liquid in beaker B must be given twice as much energy as the liquid in beaker A

A + 42 000 J   B + 84 000 J

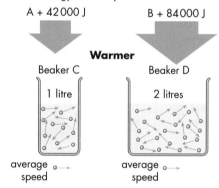

Warmer

Beaker C — 1 litre   Beaker D — 2 litres

average speed   average speed

This increases the average speed of particles in each liquid by the same amount

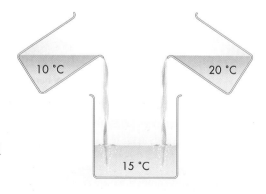

10 °C   20 °C

15 °C

How much heat is needed?

So far we have only looked at different temperatures and the heat energy in different amounts of water. How much the temperature of a material is changed by heat energy depends on two things:

● what the material is

● how much of it there is.

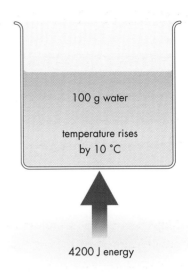

100 g water

temperature rises by 10 °C

4200 J energy

If an electric heater puts 4200 J of energy in to 100 g of water it will warm it up by 10 °C. It will take 8400 J of energy to warm 200 g of water by 10 °C. Twice as much water needs twice as much energy to raise its temperature by the same amount.

● 1 kg of water needs 4200 J of energy to raise its temperature by 1 °C.

c **How much energy is needed to increase the temperature of 1 kg of water by 5 °C?**

If you use aluminium instead of water it will need a different amount of energy to warm it by 1 °C.

● 1 kg of aluminium needs 880 J of energy to raise its temperature by 1 °C.

d **How much energy is needed to increase the temperature of 1 kg of aluminium by 5 °C?**

The total amount of heat energy in 1 kg of water and 1 kg of aluminium will be different if the temperatures are the same.

In contrast, if you transfer the same amount of heat energy to 1 kg of water and 1 kg of aluminium, the temperature change of the two will be different. It takes more energy to get the water particles vibrating faster.

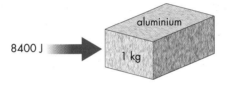

8400 J   aluminium   temperature rise of about 9.5 °C

1 kg

same energy into each material

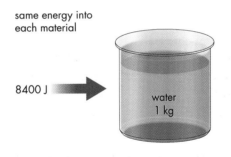

8400 J   water 1 kg   temperature rise of about 2 °C

QUESTIONS

1 What would happen to the temperature of a 1 kg block of aluminium at 50 °C if it was dropped into 1 kg of water at 20 °C? (You don't need to try to calculate the exact answer, a description will do.)

2 Why does it take far more energy to raise the temperature of a bucket of water by 10 °C than it does to raise the temperature of a cup of water by 10 °C?

3 It takes 380 J of energy to heat 1 kg of copper from 20 °C to 21 °C. Does it take more or less energy to heat the same amount of aluminium?

4 Why is it that a small block of gold will increase in temperature more than a large block of gold if the same amount of heat energy is put into both?

WHAT ARE CONDUCTORS AND INSULATORS?

Why does the handle get hot?

When you use an all metal saucepan, the handle can be cool to start with but after a while it gets hot. Heat energy from the pan is transferred along the metal handle of the saucepan, even though the handle is not above the flames. The heat energy moves from the hotter part to the cooler part. When heat energy is transferred through a material like this it is called **conduction**.

The reason why metal often feels cold to the touch of your fingers is because heat energy moves away from your fingers into the object and your fingers cool down. The metal conducts the heat away. A **conductor** is a material that allows heat to move through it fairly easily. If the object is a good heat conductor, heat moves through it quickly from a hot area to a cooler area.

You probably know that wood or polystyrene do not feel cold to touch. This is because these materials don't conduct heat so well. The heat energy will stay close to your finger and the part of the object that you are touching will warm up and not feel so cold. Materials like this are poor conductors. We call them **insulators**. An insulator is a material that only allows heat energy to move slowly through it.

How do materials conduct heat energy?

To explain how a metal saucepan handle gets hot, we need to look at a model of how the particles in a solid behave. Imagine a lot of tennis balls, each attached to its neighbours by springs. The springs represent the forces which hold particles in a solid close together. The balls can't move out of position, but they can vibrate.

If a ball on the left is shaken gently from side to side, the vibration will be passed on to the tennis balls around it. As these other tennis balls start to vibrate, they vibrate the next balls and so on. In this way the vibration moves out from the original vibrating tennis ball in all directions. The more the ball on the left is shaken, the more violent the vibration becomes.

Heat is transferred along the metal handle by conduction

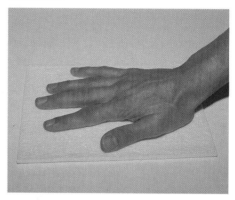
Polystyrene feels warm to the touch

ⓐ Metals are good conductors of heat. Explain why all metals feel cold to the touch even if they are at room temperature.

ⓑ Expanded polystyrene feels quite warm if you leave your hand against it for a few seconds. Is expanded polystyrene a good insulator or a good conductor?

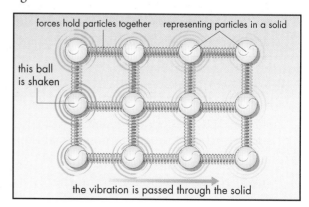
forces hold particles together   representing particles in a solid

this ball is shaken

the vibration is passed through the solid

This is very similar to the way we think heat energy is conducted through a solid. The vibration of the ball represents the heat energy coming into a material.

In solids, the closeness of the particles enable the vibrations, caused by heat energy, to move on quickly. Conduction works well in many solids because the particles are held tightly together.

In liquids, the particles move past each other and are not held tightly together so the vibrations of particles are not passed on well. This makes most liquids very poor conductors of heat.

c **Think about how the particles are arranged in a gas according to the particle theory. Do you think gases are good conductors of heat? Explain your answer.**

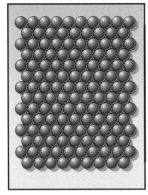

Particles in a solid are held together tightly and cannot move past each other

How do we keep warm?

Air is a gas and is a good insulator. Air is used both in nature and in man-made materials to provide insulation. Birds can reduce their heat loss in the winter by fluffing up their feathers to trap more air and provide more insulation. Duvets keep you warm at night by trapping air between the fibres. Gardeners use bubble wrap inside greenhouses to keep the heat in during winter. When you are cold you often get 'goose bumps'. The goose bumps actually make the hairs on your skin stand up. This helped to keep our hairy ancestors warm as the hairs trapped a thicker layer of air.

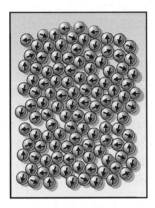

Particles in a liquid are not held tightly and so can move past each other

A bird with feathers fluffed up

Bubble wrap

QUESTIONS

1 Bicycles often have rubber grips on the handlebars. Why would your hands get colder quicker without them?

2 Why do you think the double glazing shown on the right works well as an insulator?

3 Why do you think many good insulating materials have a low density?

4 Copper is more expensive than steel, but some of the best saucepans have copper bottoms. Why do you think the manufacturers go to this expense?

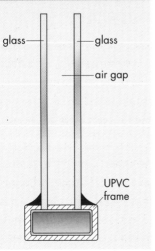

Cross-section through part of a double-glazed window

EXPANDING AND CONTRACTING

TOPIC CHECKLIST

- How do solids change when heated?
- Do all solids behave in the same way?
- Do liquids and gases expand?

How do solids change when heated?

You'll remember that a metal bar gets bigger when heated. We say it **expands**. The effect is very small and hard to see. The particles in the metal bar stay exactly the same size, but as the solid gets hotter, the particles vibrate faster and move further apart, taking up more room.

Think about people on a dance floor at a disco. If the music is slow, people move slowly and don't take up much room. As the music gets faster, the dancers move around more from side to side and jump up and down more. Each person takes up more room. The people are the same size but they take up more space in all directions.

We can show that solids expand in all directions. A brass bar is made so it just fits inside a gauge, and the end just fits through a hole in the gauge. If the bar is heated, it will expand. Now it will not fit in the gauge and cannot be pushed into the hole. When the bar cools again it **contracts** and it will fit the gauge and the hole. The bar became longer and thicker when heated because it expanded in all directions.

slow dancing –
not much space taken up

fast music and dancing –
people take up more space

The T-bar gets longer and thicker when heated

Do all solids behave in the same way?

Wall thermostats that control central heating use two thin strips of different metals stuck together like a sandwich. This is called a **bimetallic strip**. As the air gets warmer, both metal strips expand, but one expands more than the other.

As they are joined together the only way that one can expand more than the other is if they both bend. The one that expands most is on the outside of the bend. The metal strips become straight again when they cool down.

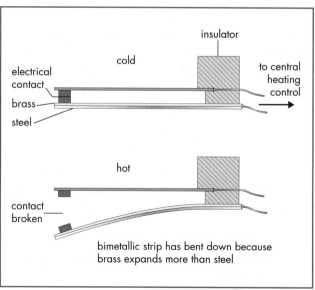

bimetallic strip has bent down because
brass expands more than steel

ⓐ Which metal in the bimetallic strip shown expands most when heated?

Lots of problems are caused by solids expanding. Bridges over motorways have expansion gaps in them to allow for the increase in length of the bridge as the bridge expands on warm days. An ordinary glass tumbler can crack if boiling water is poured into it because the part which gets hot expands and the part which is still cold does not.

Expansion gap in motorway bridge

Do liquids and gases expand?

Liquids and gases also expand when they get hot. Liquids and gases expand much more than solids.

The particles in liquids are not connected to each other and are free to move past each other. When a liquid is heated, the particles knock into each other harder and push each other further apart.

The photograph on the right shows a flask full of air with a tube sticking into a beaker of water. The ends of the tube are open.

When answering the following questions, try to use the particle model of gases.

ⓑ What will happen to the air in the flask if the person holds their hands against the flask?

ⓒ What will happen at the open end of the tube under water? Explain why.

ⓓ What will happen if the person removes their hands from the flask? Explain why.

Sealed containers often carry safety warnings about being heated, because the liquids and gases inside can try to expand and cause very high pressures. There is a risk of the containers exploding.

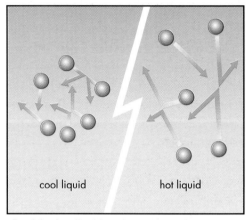

cool liquid   hot liquid

Particles in a liquid push each other further apart when they get hot

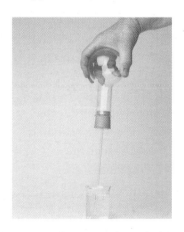

QUESTIONS

1 Which expand most, solids, liquids or gases?

2 Some people think that the particles in a solid get bigger when the material is heated. This is not true. Explain what is actually happening.

3 Railway tracks used to be made in fairly short lengths with gaps left between them. Why?

4 When overhead power lines and telephone wires are hung in the summer, some slack is left in them. Explain why.

- Why does hot air rise?
- Does convection happen in all materials?
- Where can we find convection currents?

Why does hot air rise?

You have probably seen how a helium balloon rises through the air if you let go of it. The helium and balloon together are less dense than the air around them, so the upthrust on the balloon is greater than the combined weight of the helium and balloon. An identical balloon full of air will fall in air because taken together, the air and balloon are more dense than the air around them.

You may have heard people say: 'Hot air rises' but not understood why this is. If we use the ideas of density and of things expanding when they are heated, we can explain this.

Hot-air balloons work in a similar way to helium balloons. When the air inside the hot-air balloon is heated, it expands. Some of the air is forced out of the hole in the bottom of the balloon leaving a smaller mass of air inside the balloon. The hot-air balloon is then less dense than the surrounding air so it rises.

The same thing happens in air even without a balloon. As air is heated it gets warmer and expands. The same mass of air now has a bigger volume, so the air is less dense. We know from the helium balloon that a less dense material rises through a more dense one. So like the helium balloon hot, less dense air rises through colder, more dense air. This type of movement of air and other gases due to heat is called **convection**.

helium-filled balloon rises in air

air-filled balloon falls in air

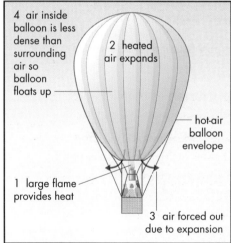

4 air inside balloon is less dense than surrounding air so balloon floats up

2 heated air expands

hot-air balloon envelope

1 large flame provides heat

3 air forced out due to expansion

expanded hot air is less dense and rises

air here gets hot and expands

ⓐ **How do you think a hot-air balloon comes back down to the ground again?**

Does convection happen in all materials?

Convection also happens in liquids. The particles in liquids and gases are free to move past each other and so particles of a liquid or gas can rise through the rest of the material.

ⓑ **Can convection currents happen in solids? Use the particle theory to explain your answer.**

We can show that convection happens in liquids using colour in water. If you drop a crystal of potassium permanganate through a straw into water, it will slowly start to dissolve and colour the water a deep purple. If one side of the base of the beaker is gently heated, the water above will be heated and rise up. The purple colour will rise with the warm water and show the movement of the water in the beaker.

If the heating continues, the coloured water rises to the top and spreads across the top. As the water moves away from the heat it cools. The particles move closer together and become more dense, so they fall again. This is called a **convection current**. The current will carry heat around the beaker, and the whole beaker of water will eventually become warm so all the water will become coloured purple.

ⓒ **If you put your hand on the top of a hot water tank it will feel hot, but at the bottom it feels cold. Why?**

ⓓ **Why do you think that putting a lid on a saucepan makes the water in it come to the boil more quickly?**

Where can we find convection currents?

Convection is happening all around us all the time. On the coast, morning breezes blow onshore and evening breezes blow offshore because the temperature change of the air is faster over the land.

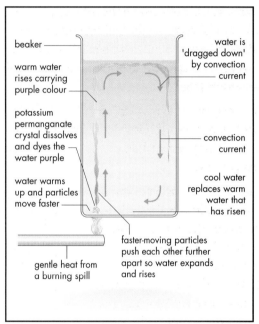

warmed water rises, carrying the purple colour with it

potassium permanganate crystal

beaker

warm water rises carrying purple colour

potassium permanganate crystal dissolves and dyes the water purple

water warms up and particles move faster

gentle heat from a burning spill

faster-moving particles push each other further apart so water expands and rises

water is 'dragged down' by convection current

convection current

cool water replaces warm water that has risen

QUESTIONS

1 Why is the heating element found at the bottom of a kettle?

2 Why is the cooling element found at the top of a fridge?

3 Why is bread usually baked in the top half of an oven?

4 Why does smoke move up a chimney?

In the morning the land and sea are both cool, but the land heats up quicker than the sea. The air over the land is warmed and rises. Cooler air from over the sea is drawn in to replace the warmed air that has risen, creating an onshore breeze. This air is also warmed and rises, and so on.

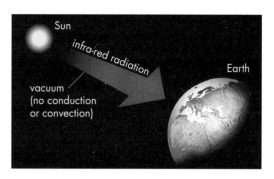

TOPIC CHECKLIST

- How do we feel heat from the Sun?
- Radiation
- Comparing all the ways heat can escape

How do we feel heat from the Sun?

The space between the Sun and Earth's atmosphere is empty. There is no matter there, no particles – it is a **vacuum**. Both conduction and convection rely on the particles in materials moving around or vibrating to transfer the heat energy. We call the material that is needed a **medium**. In the vacuum of space there are no particles to allow conduction or convection to happen.

We know that we get heat energy from the Sun. We can get a clue about how the energy travels from what happens when you use a hat to shade your head from the Sun. It stops the Sun's heat from hitting your head. The hat makes a heat shadow as well as a light shadow.

Radiation

Heat energy radiates from the Sun, and is similar to the light we see. It moves at the same speed as light, and it moves in straight lines, as light energy does. Another similarity is that light and heat energy from the Sun do not need a medium to travel through. This is how we get our heat and light energy from the Sun through the vacuum in between.

Heat energy can be reflected just like light energy. Think about the shiny mirror surface behind a light bulb in a torch. This reflects the light into a bright beam. Shiny surfaces also reflect heat and this is the reason why electric fires have a shiny metal surface behind the heating elements. It reflects the heat forward towards you.

ⓑ Why do you think the reflector behind the electric fire is curved?

There are also some differences between heat and light energy. We can see light energy but we cannot see heat energy. To see heat energy we have to use a special camera to produce a picture like the one to the right. The heat camera uses heat to form a picture in a similar way to a normal camera using light. Another difference is that light energy travels easily through glass, but most heat energy does not travel well through glass.

ⓐ If an object can form a heat shadow, what does this tell us about the way heat radiation travels?

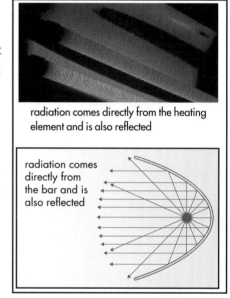

radiation comes directly from the heating element and is also reflected

radiation comes directly from the bar and is also reflected

An electric fire

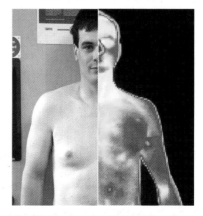

A split image using light (left) and heat (right)

Heat energy that moves without a medium has a special name – **infra-red radiation** or IR radiation. IR radiation doesn't need any particles in order for it to move. It can move through a vacuum like light can.

Some snakes use infra-red radiation to hunt in total darkness. They can sense the radiated body heat of small animals using heat sensors near their eyes.

Comparing all the ways heat can escape

Heat is transferred from a hot object to the surroundings by conduction, convection and radiation. All of these methods of heat transfer happen in the buildings we live in. As energy costs rise and energy conservation becomes crucial, ways in which we can reduce the heat lost from our buildings are becoming more important. Below are some of the more common methods of reducing heat loss from housing.

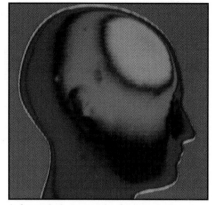

Infra-red photograph of a human head showing the hottest area in brown

c **What would be one of the disadvantages for a snake of hunting by heat alone?**

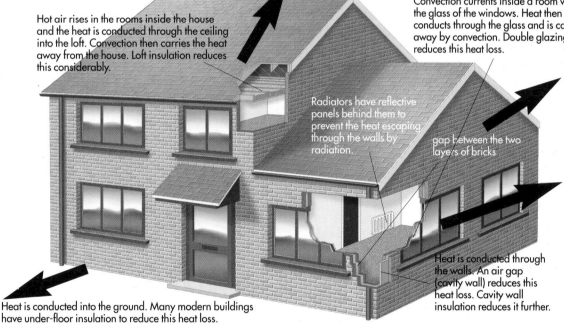

Hot air rises in the rooms inside the house and the heat is conducted through the ceiling into the loft. Convection then carries the heat away from the house. Loft insulation reduces this considerably.

Radiators have reflective panels behind them to prevent the heat escaping through the walls by radiation.

gap between the two layers of bricks

Convection currents inside a room warm the glass of the windows. Heat then conducts through the glass and is carried away by convection. Double glazing reduces this heat loss.

Heat is conducted through the walls. An air gap (cavity wall) reduces this heat loss. Cavity wall insulation reduces it further.

Heat is conducted into the ground. Many modern buildings have under-floor insulation to reduce this heat loss.

QUESTIONS

1 What is meant by the word medium?

2 Why might the space shuttle move through space with its white surface towards the Sun?

3 Which of the methods of house insulation do you think is the most cost effective? Explain your answer.

4 Double glazing is one of the most popular improvements homeowners pay for. It takes many years to get back the cost of fitting double glazing through money saved on heating bills. For what reasons other than saving energy do people choose to fit double glazing?

5 Some types of glass are coated with a layer of metal so thin that it is almost transparent. Why do the manufacturers do this?

EXPLAINING CHANGES OF STATE

What are changes of state?

The three states of matter are solid, liquid and gas. When a solid changes to a liquid, or a liquid to a gas, this is a **change of state**. These changes of state are reversible, so a gas can change to a liquid and a liquid to a solid.

The three different states of water are probably already familiar to you. Ice is solid water. It melts at its **melting point** of 0 °C and becomes liquid water. Liquid water boils at its **boiling point** of 100 °C and **evaporates** (turns from liquid to gas) to become a gas called steam. Water also **freezes** (turns from liquid to solid) at 0 °C to form ice and **condenses** (turns from gas to liquid) at 100 °C.

What happens when we heat water?

It is useful to look at a graph of the temperature change of water as it is heated from ice to liquid.

The particles in a solid, like ice, are arranged in a regular pattern, and are held tightly together. This stops them moving past each other, but it does not stop them from vibrating. If a solid is heated, the particles vibrate more and more as the material gets hotter.

When ice gets to 0 °C, the vibrations become so violent that the forces holding the particles together are not strong enough to keep them in position. As more heat energy enters the solid, more particles break free. The solid starts to melt. When the forces holding the particles together in a pattern have been overcome, the particles are free to move past each other. The solid has changed to a liquid.

When you heat a solid, something odd happens at the melting point. Before the solid reaches the melting point, the temperature rise is steady as energy is put in. Then for a while, energy is put into the solid but the temperature stays the same. This is because energy going into the solid is used to break the connections between the particles, rather than make the particles move faster. This means that the heat energy is used in melting the solid rather than raising the temperature.

The three states of water

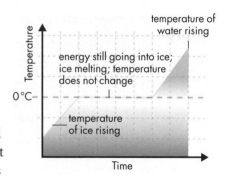

What happens to the temperature of water as it changes state

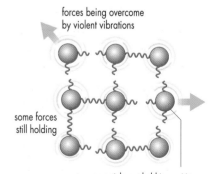

Particle model of melting

Once all the bonds are broken and all of the solid has melted to a liquid, the temperature rises once more as heat energy continues to be put into the material.

ⓐ What is the difference between ice at 0 °C and water at 0 °C?

When a liquid is heated, it gets hotter because the particles that make up the liquid move faster. When the liquid reaches the boiling point, the temperature again stops increasing.

The heat energy is now being used to separate the liquid particles and move them away from each other, until all the particles are completely free to move about. When all the liquid has become gas, further heat energy makes the gas get hotter still.

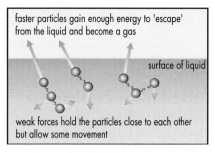
Particle model of boiling

What happens when we cool water?

When a gas cools it condenses to form a liquid. This happens at the boiling point. As heat energy leaves the gas it cools until it reaches the boiling point. Energy is leaving the gas so the particles slow down. While the gas changes to a liquid the temperature stays the same.

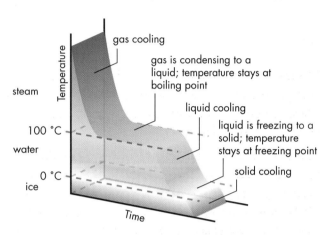
What happens to the temperature of water as it cools

When all the gas has condensed, the temperature of the liquid continues to fall until it reaches the melting point. The particles arrange themselves into a solid and forces once more hold them tightly in place. The temperature stays the same while the material solidifies. As energy continues to leave the solid it cools further.

Evaporation at low temperatures

Even when water is well below boiling point, some of the particles of water will escape from the surface and become gas. If we think back to the particle model of a liquid, we remember that some particles are moving faster than others. It is these 'hotter' particles that escape. This is called **evaporation**. Because the fastest particles leave the liquid, the average speed of the particles left behind becomes lower. This means that the liquid left behind becomes cooler.

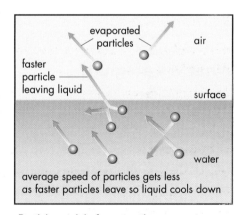
Particle model of evaporation

ⓑ Puddles on tarmac disappear but they do not boil – what is happening?

QUESTIONS

1 Imagine you are a molecule of water. Describe what happens to you as you are put into a kettle and a cup of coffee is made with you. What might happen to some of your friends?

2 If you wet the back of your hand and then blow on it, it feels cold. Why?

J Magnets and electromagnets

WHAT CAN A MAGNET DO?

Magnets attract some metals...

What do we already know about magnets?

Magnets are everyday objects, but in fact are quite mysterious. They pull some materials towards them. Sometimes they push materials away from them. They have no affect on some materials.

Some metals are affected by a magnet, but some metals are not. You may find it hard to predict which metals are affected by magnets.

What is a magnet?

A magnet is often made of iron. We can think of a bar of iron as being made up of lots of tiny magnets. Normally these magnets are not arranged in an organised way. The small magnetic effect of each tiny magnet is lost because they are all pointing in different directions. If we can arrange most or all of the little magnets so that they point in the same direction, they work together and the iron has an overall magnetic effect.

Any magnet will pull, or **attract**, iron objects towards it. It will also pull steel, which is made mostly from iron. Nickel and cobalt are also magnetic. Aluminium is one of the many metals that are not magnetic.

The most common magnets are long bars called **bar magnets**. The magnetic force is strongest at the ends, which we call the poles. One end is called the **north pole** of the magnet and the other the **south pole**. The photograph shows a bar magnet with the ends labelled N for north pole and S for South pole. All magnets have N and S poles whatever their shape, but they are not usually labelled.

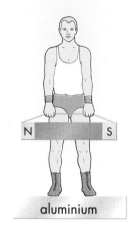

...but not others

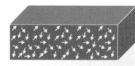

tiny magnets disorganised – no overall magnetic effect

tiny magnets organised – iron is magnetised

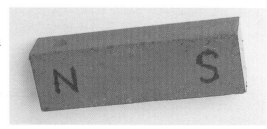

A bar magnet

How do magnets affect each other?

If you put two bar magnets on a desk, they will either **attract** each other, or **repel**, push each other away. The diagram on the right shows how a north pole will attract a south pole but repel another north pole. Similarly, a south pole will attract a north pole but repel a south pole. These forces increase if the magnets are closer to each other and decrease if the magnets are further apart.

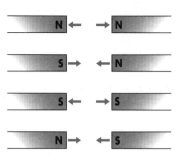

Like poles repel; unlike poles attract

ⓐ **When you pull two magnets apart, how does the force between them change as they get further apart?**

Which is a magnet and which a magnetic material?

Because magnets can be repelled as well as attracted to other magnets, we can sort magnets from magnetic materials.

The picture shows three objects, two are magnets and one is a piece of steel. Each magnet has two poles. Both poles of both magnets attract the steel object but one end of one magnet will repel one end of the other magnet.

The only way to be sure a material is a magnet is to test not for attraction, but for repulsion. If the magnet repels an object, then the object is also a magnet. In this case object B is the block of steel as A and C repel each other.

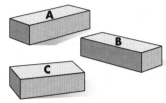

both ends of A always attract B
both ends of C always attract B
each end of A attracts one end of C
and repels the other end

Can materials become magnetic?

Can materials become magnetic?

Iron and steel are the most common magnetic materials, and are easily magnetised. If you take a needle and stroke a strong magnet along it several times in the same direction, the needle will become magnetised. The stroking 'organises' the magnetic particles inside the needle.

When are magnets useful?

Magnets have a wide range of uses, including: holding messages on fridge doors; keeping the pieces in place in travel games such as chess, noughts and crosses; picking up pins; sorting steel from aluminium; sensors in burglar alarms; keeping doors closed.

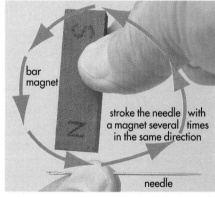

bar magnet

stroke the needle with a magnet several times in the same direction

needle

Making a magnet by stroking with another magnet

ⓑ **How does a fridge magnet hold a message on the fridge door?**

QUESTIONS

1 The drawing on the right represents three bar magnets. Copy the drawing and add N and S for the north and south poles so that all ends of the magnets are attracting each other.

2 Which of the following will a magnet attract?
nickel plastic iron cobalt aluminium steel

3 Magnets are used to sort steel and aluminium cans. Explain how this works.

4 Steel can be magnetised using a magnet. Heat makes particles vibrate and rearrange themselves. Why do you think steel can be demagnetised if it is heated?

N

What is a magnetic field?

We have learned that magnets produce forces at their poles. In fact, the force of the magnet has an effect in the space around it. This is called a **magnetic field**. Magnetic fields are invisible but their shape can be shown using iron filings. If you put a thin piece of card on top of a bar magnet and sprinkle fine iron filings onto the card, the magnetic field of the magnet will make the iron filings move into a pattern.

How does a compass work?

A compass is in fact a small bar magnet, mounted on a pin, so that it can turn. You can use a small compass called a plotting compass to show a magnetic field. As with the iron filings the compass needle turns to show where the magnetic field is. We show the magnetic field by drawing **magnetic field lines**. We draw the field lines with arrows on them to show which way the north pole of a compass would point.

The diagram shows the magnetic field lines of a bar magnet. Notice that the lines of magnetic force never cross or touch. They lead between the north pole and the south pole of the magnet.

The magnetic field is strongest where the lines are closest together. This happens close to the poles. It explains why the pull of a magnet gets weaker as you move further from the magnet – the lines are spreading out.

ⓐ **Which way does the arrow on a magnetic field line point, towards north or south?**

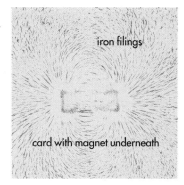

Iron filings show the magnetic field of a magnet

A plotting compass

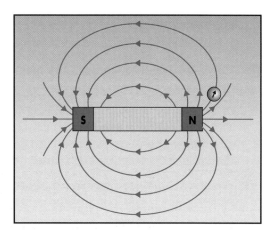

The field lines of a bar magnet

Field lines between magnets

When two magnets attract each other, they change each other's magnetic field patterns. The magnetic field lines show the force of the field goes from the north pole to the south pole. Notice the field lines are close together near to the ends of the magnets. This shows the force here is strong.

When two magnets repel each other, again they change the shape of each other's magnetic fields. This time, they seem to 'push' each other's field lines away. Notice that there is a small area between the poles where there are no magnetic field lines. Here there is no magnetic force.

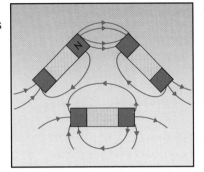

ⓑ Copy the diagram and add the missing pole labels to the magnets.

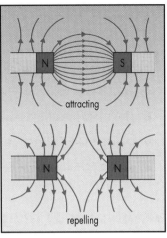

Magnetic field lines between magnets

Can magnetic fields act through materials?

You can use a magnet to attach a message on a piece of paper to the fridge. The magnetic force can act through the paper, but is this true for all materials?

You can test this in the lab using a magnet and a paper clip. The magnet is held in a clamp, and the paper clip is tied with a length of cotton to the bench. The first photograph below shows a piece of paper between them. The paper clip is being held up by the attraction of a magnet held above it. The magnetic force works through the paper, as though the paper wasn't there.

The second photograph shows a sheet of aluminium in between the magnet and the paper clip. The magnetic field acts through the aluminium.

The third photograph shows a sheet of steel placed between the magnet and the paper clip. The paper clip has fallen to the ground. The magnetic field is screened by the sheet of steel. This effect can be used as a test for magnetic properties. If the sheet screens the magnetic field, then the material the sheet is made from has magnetic properties.

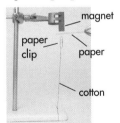

Magnetic force works through paper

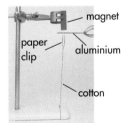

Magnetic force works through aluminium

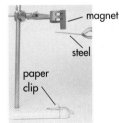

The steel has 'screened' the magnetic force

ⓒ What do you think would happen to the paper clip if you put a sheet of plastic between it and the magnet?

QUESTIONS

1 We use iron filings to show the pattern of magnetic fields. Why won't aluminium filings work?

2 Magnets attract steel. Why, then, is a compass needle affected by a piece of steel if the steel is not magnetised?

3 Where is the magnetic field of a bar magnet strongest?

4 Give two reasons why a paper clip is used in the experiment shown on this page.

TOPIC CHECKLIST

- Which way do magnets point on the Earth?
- Are magnetic fields flat?
- Using the Earth's magnetic field
- When don't compasses work?

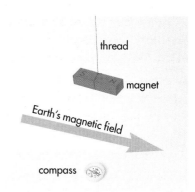

Which way do magnets point on the Earth?

If a magnet is allowed to turn freely it will always end up pointing in the same direction. It turns out that this direction is north/south. This is because the Earth has its own magnetic effect which extends above the surface of the Earth. It is called the **Earth's magnetic field**.

Imagine the Earth with a giant bar magnet inside it. We know that the 'north' end of a compass needle points towards the north pole of the Earth. As north poles are attracted to south poles, this means our imaginary giant bar magnet inside the Earth must have its south pole in the place we call the North Pole. The north magnetic pole of our imaginary magnet is in the Antarctic or the place we call the South Pole.

a Which chemical element inside the Earth do you think is responsible for the Earth's magnetic field?

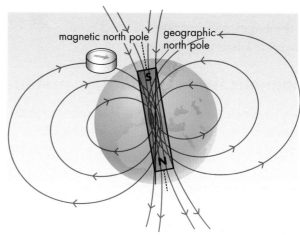

The Earth's magnetic field

Are magnetic fields flat?

We showed the magnetic field of a bar magnet on a flat piece of card. In fact, magnetic fields are three-dimensional.

This is also true of the Earth's magnetic field. The diagram shows how the magnetic field lines surround the Earth. You can see from the diagram that at the North or South Pole, a bar magnet would point straight down to the centre of the Earth.

b Explain why a compass would not be very useful near the North or South Pole.

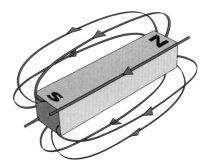

A bar magnet's magnetic field in three dimensions

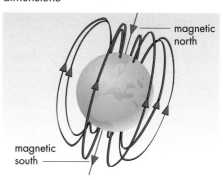

The Earth has a three-dimensional magnetic field

Using the Earth's magnetic field

The effect of the Earth's magnetic field has long been known and has been used for navigation on the sea since the 11th century. Lodestone is a rock containing iron which is a natural magnet and can be used to make compasses. These days, ships and aircraft use compasses so that they know in which direction they are travelling. People used to navigate by the stars or the Sun, but the advantage of a compass is that you can use it in the dark and at cloudy times and even in thick fog.

Lodestone is magnetic

Some birds seem to be able to navigate using the Earth's magnetic field. Even some bacteria detect the magnetic field of the Earth and move along it.

Walkers use compasses to help them find their way on the hills, especially in bad weather conditions of rain, fog or snow.

When don't compasses work?

From the paper clip experiment we have learnt that magnetic materials change the magnetic fields around them. If you put a compass on your desk and then bring a piece of steel near it, the compass needle will move and no longer point north. When you take the steel away the compass will once again point north/south.

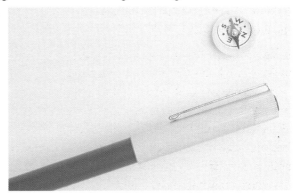

People using a compass out in the countryside need to move away from steel fences or buildings which may contain steel, to make sure their compass works accurately. There are areas, such as Dartmoor and Scotland, where the rocks contain a lot of iron. This can also stop a compass working accurately.

The steel in the pen deflects the compass needle

QUESTIONS

1 Walkers on Dartmoor might raise and lower their compass over the ground to see if the needle changes direction. Why do they do this? Explain your answer.

2 For a compass to work, the compass needle must be allowed to turn with very little friction, why must the friction be so low?

3 The housings of compasses on ships are very often made of brass or bronze. Bronze and brass look attractive and do not rust. What other property do these metals have that makes them suitable to hold a compass?

4 Much of the Viking exploration by sea before 1000 AD was done keeping the coast of Europe in sight. Why do you think this was?

HOW CAN ELECTRICITY MAKE A MAGNET?

Does electric current have a magnetic effect?

An electric current flowing through a wire creates a magnetic field around the wire. You can see this by putting a single wire vertically down through a piece of card and sprinkling iron filings on the card. The iron filings arrange themselves in a series of circles centred on the wire. The field lines are circular. In fact, the magnetic field lines around a wire are like a series of tubes. To increase the strength of the magnetic field, we can increase the electric current flowing through the wire.

If you use plotting compasses to plot the magnetic field it will also show you a circular magnetic field. If you swap the direction of the electric current, the compass will point in the opposite direction.

Coiling the wire increases the strength of the magnetic field. The photograph at the bottom of the page shows a single wire and a coil of wire using the same current. Notice how much more strongly the iron filings are showing the circular pattern of the magnetic field around the coil.

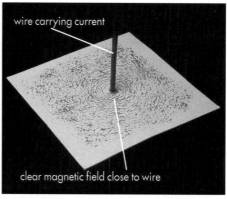

The magnetic field around a wire

What is an electromagnet?

A coil of wire with a current flowing through it has a magnetic effect, but the magnetic field it produces is fairly weak. If you put a core of magnetic material inside the coils it increases the strength of the magnetic field enormously. This is called an **electromagnet**.

The best material to use for a core is soft iron. It is easily magnetised, but also loses its magnetism again when the current in the coil is turned off. The fact that the magnetic effect stops when the current is turned off is one of the advantages of an electromagnet.

As current flows through the coils, a magnetic field is produced. This organises the tiny magnets within the iron, which makes the magnetic field stronger. When the current is turned off, the organisation is lost and the soft iron loses its magnetism.

Magnetic field lines around a coil

A coil of wire has a greater magnetic effect than a single wire

Steel is a magnetic material which could be used in the core of a coil. However, when the electric current is switched off, the steel stays magnetic. In situations where you want to be able to turn a magnet on and off, a soft iron core is better.

As we have seen, a core inside a coil increases the strength of the magnetic field. There are two other ways of increasing the magnetic effect of a coil.

The photographs show the three ways of making the magnetic effect of a current-carrying coil stronger. As well as using a core, you can increase the current or increase the number of turns in the coil.

no core
0.2 A
40 coils

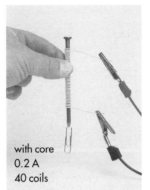
with core
0.2 A
40 coils

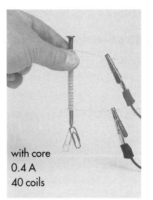
with core
0.4 A
40 coils

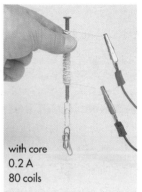
with core
0.2 A
80 coils

Different ways of making an electromagnet stronger

What are electromagnets used for?

Using an electromagnet, it is possible to get a stronger magnetic effect than with a magnet. This means electromagnets can be used to lift heavy items such as cars. Because the magnetic effect stops when the current is switched off, then the car can be put down again.

Many blocks of flats have front door locks that can be operated by people from inside their flats. When they press a button, an electric current flows and creates a magnetic field in a coil of wire buried in the door frame. The magnetic field pulls a soft iron core into the coils and unlocks the door. When the button is released, the magnetic field disappears and the lock closes again.

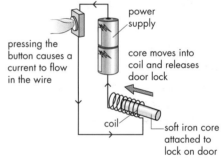
power supply
pressing the button causes a current to flow in the wire
core moves into coil and releases door lock
coil
soft iron core attached to lock on door

A solenoid door lock

ⓐ Explain why an electromagnet with a steel core would not be useful for lifting cars.

QUESTIONS

1 What are the three ways of making an electromagnet stronger?

2 Copper wire is not a magnetic material, so why is it useful in an electromagnet?

3 Electromagnets are used to pick up scrap metal. What is the advantage of this over using a large, permanent magnet?

4 Which of the following objects would make the best core for an electromagnet? Explain your answer.
steel needle   aluminium rod   soft iron nail   plastic ruler

K Light

HOW DOES LIGHT TRAVEL?

> **TOPIC CHECKLIST**
>
> ● Where does light come from?
> ● How fast does light travel?
> ● Does light travel in straight lines or curves?
> ● How can we represent the way light travels?

Where does light come from?

Light is a form of energy, so it is not surprising that very hot things, which have lots of heat energy, also give off light. Something that gives off light is called a **source** of light. The Sun is perhaps the most obvious light source – an enormous ball of hot gases. Other sources of light that you may think of are light bulbs, flames in fires or flames of candles. They all give out light energy. You may notice that they also give out heat.

Light travels in straight lines

Light does not need a material or **medium** to travel through. Light, like heat radiation, travels best through a vacuum, although it also travels well in glass, air and water. On its journey from the Sun to the Earth, light travels through the vacuum of space.

How fast does light travel?

Light travels about 300 000 000 metres in one second. That means that light from the UK would get across to the United States of America in just over one hundredth of a second. Light from the Sun reaches us in about 8.5 minutes.

You will have already done some work on the Solar System and the stars in our galaxy. The distances between stars are so enormous that the measurement, **light year**, is used as a more convenient unit for distance than metres or kilometres. So, in one year, light travels one light year or 9 460 000 000 000 km. The closest star outside our Solar System is about 4 light years away.

ⓐ How long would it take light to get to the Moon and back? (The Moon orbits the Earth at a distance of 385 000 000 m.)

Does light travel in straight lines or curves?

Light almost always travels in straight lines, which is why **shadows** are formed. Where an object blocks light there is a shadow. The fact that light moves in straight lines gives the shadow a sharp edge.

light

shadow

screen

In the diagram on the right there are three cards. Each card has two holes in it. The ones on the right are in a straight line and the ones on the left are not. A straight light beam would pass through the three holes that line up as shown by the light from source **A**. To check that light moves in a straight line we can move one of the holes out of line and see what happens. This is shown by the light from source **B**. We use three holes because two holes are always in a straight line but three holes have to line up.

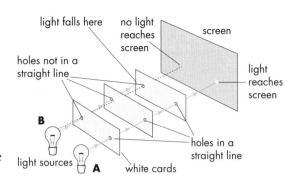

How can we represent the way light travels?

Light from a bulb moves outwards from the bulb in straight lines, in all directions. We can represent the light from the bulb by lots of arrows. The diagram might look like the one on the previous page which is rather complicated to make sense of.

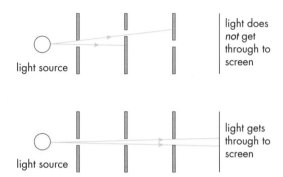

To work out what happens to the light as it travels, we need to simplify the situation a little. So instead of drawing lots of light rays, we draw only those which are important for what we are looking at. The arrows show which way the light is travelling. We call this a **ray diagram**.

To study how light behaves, we often use equipment which produces a single ray of light. The sort of equipment used is shown in the photograph on the right. Drawing the ray diagram then simply becomes a tracing of the path of the single light ray.

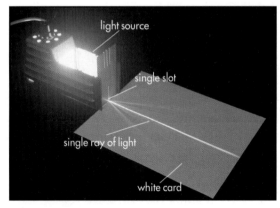

A ray box

QUESTIONS

1 How far does light move in **a** 10 seconds? **b** 1000 years?

2 Light years are used for measuring the distance between stars, instead of kilometres. Why is this?

3 For most measurements, scientist assume light takes no time to move from one place in the laboratory to another. Why is it reasonable to assume this for most experiments in the lab?

4 Astronomers sometimes talk about looking back in time when they study different stars. What do they mean by this?

TOPIC CHECKLIST

● Can light travel through materials?

● Investigating transmission, absorption and reflection

Can light travel through materials?

Light can travel through some materials. This is called **transmission**. Materials that are **transparent**, like plain glass, transmit light in an organised way so that we can see the details of an object through the material.

Other materials are **translucent**, which means that although the light rays get through, they are **scattered** as they pass through the material. The information the light carries becomes confused. Some windows made of glass or plastic are translucent. They can allow daylight into a house for people to see by, but stop people outside seeing details inside the house.

Some materials let no light through. They are **opaque**. This is for one of two reasons – either the material **reflects** the light, for example a shiny metal surface, or the material **absorbs** the light energy and transforms it into heat. Opaque materials usually reflect *and* absorb light. All metals are opaque; bricks and wood are also opaque.

When light is reflected off a surface, the light either bounces off in an organised way as it does off a mirror, or the light is scattered. Smooth surfaces reflect in an organised way and matt surfaces like paper, scatter the light.

ⓐ Why can't you see your reflection in a piece of paper even though it reflects light?

Normally we think of glass as totally transparent, but in fact some light is reflected at the surface of glass and some light is absorbed when it passes through the glass. Water behaves in the same way.

ⓑ Water is transparent, so why is it dark on the sea bed?

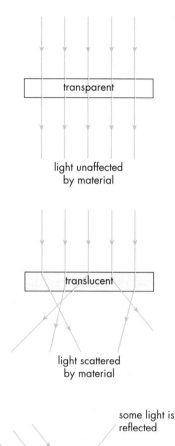

transparent

light unaffected by material

translucent

light scattered by material

some light is reflected

some light is absorbed

opaque

no light is transmitted

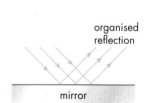

organised reflection

mirror

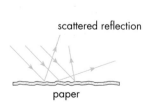

scattered reflection

paper

Investigating transmission, absorption and reflection

To find out how good a reflector a material is, we can measure the amount of light bouncing off a surface with a light sensor. The table shows the light level reflected by each material.

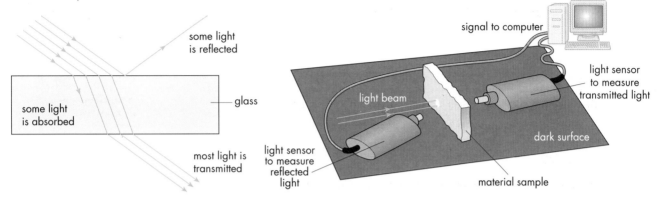

You can use the same equipment to measure the transmission of light by the material by measuring how much light comes through the material.

	Control (no material)	Glass	Wood	Paper	Cotton wool
Transmitted (%)	100	95	0	30	15
Reflected (%)	0	3	17	25	20

If you add together the reflected and transmitted values for each material and compare these with the control data, where there was no material in the way, you will find there is some 'missing' light. This light was either absorbed or scattered.

If you compare the light sensor readings with the control experiment where no material was in the way, you can work out how much of the light is reflected or transmitted by the material.

c Using the data in the table, list the materials in order of reflection with the best first.

d Use the data in the table to name the material which is best at transmitting light.

e From the information in the table, work out which material probably absorbs the most light.

QUESTIONS

1 Glass absorbs some light, so why do we call it transparent?

2 Why does a rough surface like paper scatter reflected light rather than reflecting it in an organised way?

3 Mirrors are good reflectors. Make a list of five other things that reflect light well.

4 Black cats are good light absorbers. Make a list of five other things you think are good absorbers.

5 Look at the list of absorbers you have made for question 4. How do you know they are good absorbers?

TOPIC CHECKLIST

- How do we see things?
- What does your eye do?

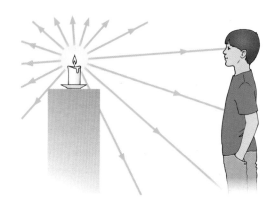

How do we see things?

If you look at a light bulb or a television screen, you see the light they are giving out. Light travels in straight lines and enters your eye. Sources of light are **luminous** because they give out light.

Many objects are not sources of visible light, but we see them by the light they reflect. They are **non-luminous**. The reason you can see the page you are reading is because you see the light reflected off the page. We only see the Moon and planets because they reflect the light from the Sun.

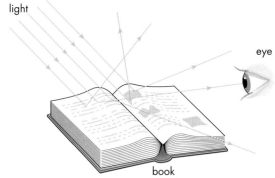

light

eye

book

ⓐ On a very clear night you can sometimes see the 'dark' side of the Moon very faintly lit. How is the light getting to the side of the Moon which is away from the Sun?

What does your eye do?

The light from luminous objects or the reflected light from non-luminous objects has to enter your eye for you to see anything. The human eye is rather like a camera. The most simple form of camera is a pinhole camera.

You can see from the diagram how the light rays make an image of the arrow inside the camera. You will notice that the image inside the camera is upside down. This is because the light rays from the top and the bottom of an object cross over to form an image on the screen.

Your eye is fantastically complex and allows you to see in a wide variety of conditions.

- The light passes in through a hole called the **pupil**. The pupil can change size and let in more or less light.

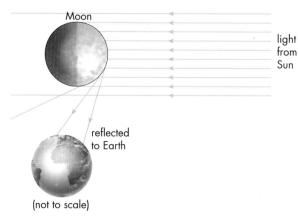

Moon

light from Sun

reflected to Earth

(not to scale)

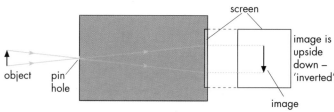

object   pin hole

screen

image is upside down – 'inverted'

image

How a pinhole camera works

- At the back of your eye there is a layer of cells called the **retina** which is light sensitive. This means that when light touches the cells they send an electrical signal to your brain.

- The **lens** compensates for things that are far away or very close by changing its shape, making the image on the back of the eye in focus.

- The light changes direction at the surface of the **cornea** and at both surfaces of the lens.

- Just as with the pinhole camera, you can see from the diagram that the image inside the eye is upside down, but the brain translates it for you so you 'see' it the right way up.

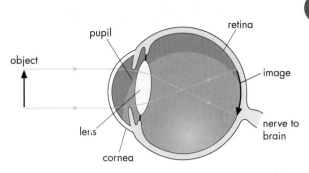

How the human eye works

ⓑ Make a list of similarities in the pinhole camera and the eye.

We can understand a lot more about how images are formed by making a few simple changes to the pinhole camera. If we have three pinholes instead of one, then three images are formed. The images are all upside down but the pattern of the images is exactly the same as the pattern of the pinholes. This is because the light rays cross over to form each image but the light from each hole forms a separate image.

If the pinhole is made bigger, then the image becomes much brighter, but it also becomes fuzzy. This is because light rays from lots of places are able to reach each point on the screen and 'confuse' the image.

If a lens is used, the brightness of the light stays the same, but the image becomes sharp again. This is exactly what happens in your eye. As the pupil gets bigger (in dim conditions) then the image tends to become fuzzy. The lens in your eye makes the image sharp again.

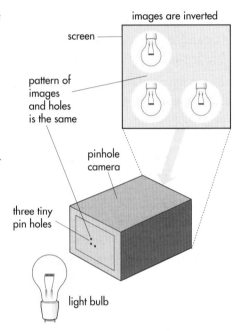

A large hole gives a fuzzy image

A lens gives a sharp image

QUESTIONS

1 Make a list of five luminous objects.

2 Why does your pupil get bigger when it is dark?

3 What is the name of the layer of light-sensitive cells on the back of your eye?

4 Explain why the image in your eye is upside down.

5 Why do you need a lens in your eye?

HOW DOES LIGHT REFLECT?

What happens to reflected light?

Light moves in straight lines and when it hits a flat, smooth, shiny surface it bounces off in an organised way and travels in a straight line away from the surface. A plane mirror has a flat, smooth, shiny surface.

incident ray   reflected ray

mirror surface

A light ray coming towards a surface is called an **incident ray**. The light ray which is reflected is called the **reflected ray**.

The diagrams show that the direction that the reflected ray will travel in depends on the direction the incident ray came from. If a light ray hits a mirror

at 90° to the surface as in **A**, the light is reflected straight back in exactly the direction it came from. Scientists call this line the **normal**. If the light ray hits the mirror slightly to the left of the normal, it will be reflected back just to the right of the normal. This is shown in **B** and **C**.

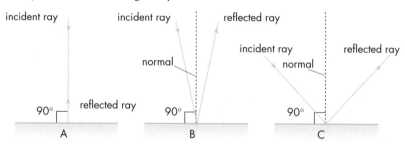

Reflection at a flat, shiny surface

We can measure the angle between the incident ray and the normal, and the angle between the reflected ray and the normal. The angle between the incident ray and the normal is called the **angle of incidence.** The angle between the reflected ray and the normal is called the **angle of reflection**.

a **What do you notice about the way the rays are reflected at the surface of the mirror?**

Is there a link between angle of incidence and angle of reflection?

If you look closely at the three diagrams of reflected light rays, you can see that the angle of reflection is always equal to the angle of incidence.

The ray diagram on the right shows the angles of incidence and reflection.
The angle of incidence is labelled *i* and the angle of reflection is labelled *r*.

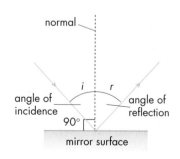

b **If the angle of reflection is 35°, what is the angle of incidence?**

How are reflected images formed?

When you look in a mirror you see your reflection. If you look at writing in a mirror, it appears reversed. Ambulances have the word AMBULANCE in 'mirror writing' on the front of them so that drivers see the word the right way round in their rear view mirrors. Some words and letters are symmetrical and look the same in a mirror as they do normally.

c Make a list of letters from the alphabet that are symmetrical.

d Write down four symmetrical words.

The letters appear back to front but not upside down. If you write the letter F on a clear plastic sheet and then turn the sheet over, the F looks back to front. This is called **lateral inversion**. This is what is happening in the mirror. To see an F on a piece of paper reflected in a mirror, you need to turn the paper to face away from you, so the letter appears laterally inverted.

The F on the paper is written correctly but the reflection is laterally inverted

Multiple reflections

If you put two mirrors at an angle to each other so that they form a corner, you can see more than one reflection of an object between them. In fact, as the angle changes between them, the number of images changes. This is how a kaleidoscope works. You may have looked at yourself in mirrors like this.

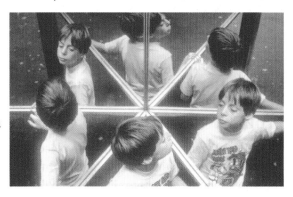

The table on the right shows the angle between two mirrors and the number of images you can see.

e What happens to the number of reflected images as the angle between the two mirrors increases?

Angle (°)	Number of images
45	7
60	5
90	3
120	2

QUESTIONS

1 Draw an accurate ray diagram for the light reflected from a plane mirror when the angle of incidence is 40 degrees. Label all the angles and the normal.

2 Draw an accurate ray diagram for the light reflected from a plane mirror when the angle of incidence is 73 degrees. Label all the angles and the normal.

3 Approximately what angle would you need between two mirrors to give you nine reflected images?

HOW CAN WE CHANGE COLOUR?

How do filters change white light?

If we shine white light through a green filter, green light comes through. Filters affect the colour of light we see. A green filter lets green light through but will absorb the other colours. The green filter **transmits** only green light. Each filter transmits its own colour of light. So what happens when we try to pass sunlight through more than one colour filter?

If white light shines onto a filter that only transmits green, the green light goes through. If the green light then hits a red filter, no light goes through. The red filter only lets red light through and this has already been absorbed by the green filter.

ⓐ **What colour light is transmitted by a blue filter?**

ⓑ **What colour light is transmitted by a red and a blue filter together?**

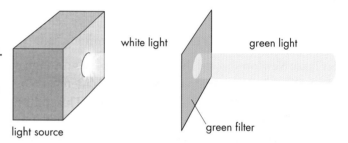

A green filter absorbs all other colours and transmits green light

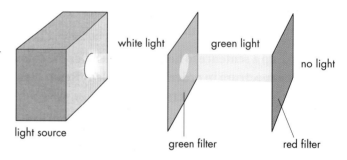

If two different coloured filters are used, no light passes through

Can we make new colours?

There are three **primary** colours – red, blue and green. These can be added together to form any other colour of light, including white. For example, if primary red light and primary blue light are shone onto a white screen, they form magenta light where the patches of light overlap. You can see this in the diagram on the right.

The three **primary** colours can be mixed in many combinations to form any of the other colours of the spectrum.

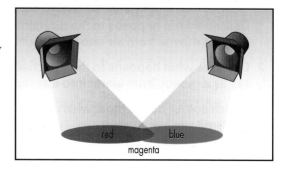

The chart on the right shows the colours you get when red, green and blue are mixed in equal amounts.

c What colours of light must you mix to get yellow?

Why do things look coloured?

When you see a red ball, it looks red because it is reflecting mostly red light. White light hits the ball but the other colours are absorbed by the ball and only the red light is reflected (Picture **a**). Objects look whichever colour they reflect.

If an object's colour is made up from two primary colours, it must reflect both colours. A yellow flower reflects mostly green and red light (Picture **b**). The colour you see is yellow.

What happens if we look at things in coloured light?

If we look at a red ball in red light it looks red. If we look at a green ball in red light it will look black because there is no green light for it to reflect and it absorbs the red light. If we look at a white ball in red light it looks red because it cannot reflect colours that are not there.

d What colour will a blue dress look in red light?

e What colour will a yellow shirt look in red light?

How do televisions show colours?

Television screens contain thousands of spots of a chemical that glows when hit by electrons. The spots are arranged in groups of three, with each spot glowing a different colour. The more energy the spot gets from the electrons, the brighter the spot glows. By controlling the mix of energy going to the spots, the colours on the television screen are changed.

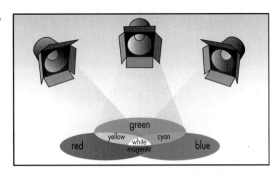

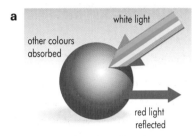

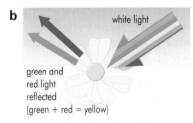

a

Why a red ball is red

b

Why a yellow flower is yellow

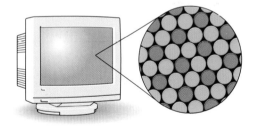

QUESTIONS

1 Which are the three primary colours of light?

2 Which colours of light must you add to get magenta?

3 If you look at a red pen mark on a white page through a red filter you will not see the mark. Why?

4 Street lights give out a single orange colour. What colour will a car look if it doesn't normally reflect orange?

L Sound and hearing

HOW ARE DIFFERENT SOUNDS MADE?

> **TOPIC CHECKLIST**
>
> - How are sounds made?
> - Seeing the vibration
> - How high or low?
> - How loud or soft?

How are sounds made?

When something moves backwards and forwards quickly, we say it is **vibrating**. Things that vibrate make sounds. The sound made is a form of energy that has been transformed from the movement energy of the vibrating object. A bee flying by makes a distinctive buzzing sound. The sound comes from the bee's wings moving backwards and forwards very fast. The wings move so fast that you can't see them move.

Musical instruments also have parts which vibrate. The part that vibrates depends on the type of instrument:

- Stringed instruments make a sound because the strings vibrate. The length, thickness and tension in the string all affect the sound.

- The skin on a drum vibrates when you hit it. The tightness and thickness of the skin affect the sound.

- Blowing into a recorder makes the air inside it vibrate. By covering up different holes different sounds can be made.

Seeing the vibration

If you take a tuning fork and strike it gently on a wood block, you can hear it 'sing'. You may be able to see that the fork looks blurred because it is moving very quickly.

If you move the tuning fork up to a ping-pong ball, the ball suddenly moves as it is hit by the tuning fork moving backwards and forwards quickly. A tuning fork can also be made to make ripples on water.

How high or low?

The **pitch** of a note is how high or low the note is. The pitch depends on how fast something vibrates. The number of vibrations made each second is called the **frequency**. Frequency has a special unit called hertz, which can be written 'Hz'.

A high-pitch note has a high frequency and is caused by something vibrating fast. A low-pitch note has a low frequency and is caused by something vibrating slowly.

The pitch of a note can be changed by making the vibrations quicker or slower. There are three ways of making a string vibrate more quickly:

● make the string shorter ● make the string tighter ● use a lighter string.

The same ideas can be applied to a drum. The tighter the skin is pulled, the higher the pitch of the sound. Big drums make lower pitched sounds and a thinner skin raises the pitch.

ⓐ **What three ways are there of causing a string on a guitar to make a lower note?**

ⓑ **Organ pipes work like recorders, but come in different lengths. Explain how they make different notes.**

A cathode ray oscilloscope (CRO) shows a 'picture' of sound vibrations. Sound is picked up by a microphone and turned into electrical signals. These signals can be seen on the CRO screen. The diagram shows high and low sounds on a CRO.

How loud or soft?

Loud sounds have big vibrations and quiet sounds have small ones. **Amplitude** is the loudness of the sound. A loud sound has a big amplitude. To make a louder sound using a double bass, the string must be plucked harder. This makes the string move further.

ⓒ **How would you make a quiet note on a double bass?**

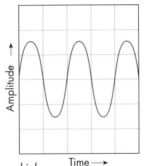
high . . . Time →

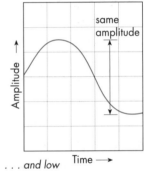
same amplitude
. . . and low Time →

Loudness is often measured in **decibels** by sound meters. Some examples of loudness are shown in the table opposite. The diagram shows loud and quiet sounds on a CRO.

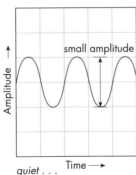
small amplitude
quiet . . . Time →

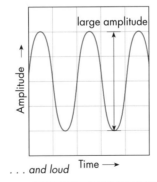
large amplitude
. . . and loud Time →

Sound	Loudness (decibels)
whispering	10
wind in leaves	17
waves on beach	40
shouting	70
vacuum cleaner	80
loud music	100
aircraft engines	110

QUESTIONS

1 How loud are jet engines?

2 Why are different thicknesses of wire used for guitar strings?

3 a Middle C on a piano produces 256 vibrations in one second. Would a higher pitch note have fewer, the same, or more vibrations in a second?

b How many vibrations per second would a quiet middle C on the piano have?

HOW DOES SOUND TRAVEL THROUGH SOLIDS LIQUIDS AND GASES?

Does sound need a medium?

Most of the time sound travels from something making a sound, through the air around us, to our ears. Sound vibrations need a material to travel through. The material is called the **medium**. If there is no medium, vibrations cannot reach us. A space with nothing in it is called a **vacuum**.

The photograph at the top shows a glass jar which has had the air taken out of it. The electric bell inside is vibrating, but you would not hear any sound coming out of the jar because there is no air to vibrate and transfer the sound vibrations.

How does sound travel through a gas?

The particles in air carry the sound vibrations through changes in pressure. This is shown in the diagram on the right. Sound travels slower in gas than in liquids and solids because the particles are further apart so they collide less often.

How does sound travel through a liquid?

Fish rely very heavily on vibrations for hearing. Although they do not have ears, they sense the vibrations in the water. Other sea creatures, such as dolphins, use underwater sound to communicate with each other. It is thought that whales can use low-frequency sound to communicate around the world.

Sound travels even better in water than it does in air. This is because the particles in water are much closer together than in a gas, and so the vibrations can be transferred more quickly and effectively.

The sound wave creates areas of higher pressure where the particles are closer together . . .

Sound pressure waves move away from the source.

sound source

. . . and areas of lower pressure where the particles are further apart.

Sound waves in air

The particles in a liquid are close together so they pass on pressure waves more quickly.

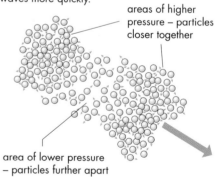

areas of higher pressure – particles closer together

area of lower pressure – particles further apart

Sound waves in water

Two experimenters used a bell and stopwatch to measure the speed of sound in water. One of them hit the bell under the water at one side of a lake; the other started the stopwatch when he saw the bell hit. He stopped the watch when he heard the sound of the bell under water. Light gets across a lake in a fraction of a millionth of a second.

a **Why would this experiment not work in a swimming pool?**

b **Would the sound of the bell get across the lake faster or slower in air?**

How does sound travel through a solid?

Sound travels faster through solids than it does through liquids and gases because the particles in a solid are close together and linked to each other, so they pass on the vibrations more quickly.

The sound of a train coming can be heard through the rails long before the train can be heard through air.

How can we measure the speed of sound?

We can measure the speed of sound by measuring the time it takes for an **echo** (sound being reflected) to come back to us. Rachel and Joey take two blocks of wood and a stopwatch outside. They stand 150 metres from a wall. Rachel bangs the two blocks of wood together and Joey times how long it takes the echo to come back to him. It takes a little under one second to come back.

$$\text{speed of sound} = \frac{\text{distance from wall} \times 2}{\text{time to hear echo}}$$

Comparing sound and light

Sound travels through air at about 300 metres per second (m/s). Light travels about 1 million times faster, at 300 000 000 m/s. We can experience this difference when a thunderstorm takes place several kilometres away. You see the flash of light and then hear the sound of thunder several seconds afterwards.

For example, if the thunder takes 15 seconds to reach you after you see the light from the lightning, the storm must be about 4.5 km away.

Distance = speed × time = 300 m/s × 15 s = 4500 m or 4.5 km.

The table compares the properties of thunder and lightning (sound and light).

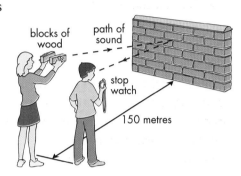

area of higher pressure – particles closer together

area of lower pressure – particles further apart

The particles in a solid are close together and linked so they pass on pressure waves very quickly.

Sound waves in a solid

blocks of wood   path of sound   stop watch   150 metres

C Why is it easier to measure long times more accurately than short times?

Thunder (sound)	Lightning (light)
travels at 300 m/s	travels at 300 000 000 m/s
needs a medium, e.g. air, to travel through	can travel through air and a vacuum
reflects off any flat, solid surfaces	reflects off light-coloured and shiny surfaces
absorbed by soft and irregular surfaces	absorbed by dark surfaces
can be heard around corners, e.g. of buildings	can only be seen if viewed directly or reflected

QUESTIONS

1 As you climb a mountain, the air gets less dense. Do you think the speed of sound changes as you climb a mountain? Explain your answer.

2 If you put your ear against a door, you can hear people talking on the other side more clearly than if you just put your ear near the door. Why is this?

3 Someone sees lightning and then hears thunder 12 second later. Calculate how far away the storm is.

4 Describe three differences between sound and light.

HOW DO WE HEAR SOUNDS?

TOPIC CHECKLIST

- How do we hear?
- What can we hear?
- Are there sounds we can't hear?

How do we hear?

The human ear is a delicate and complex system which helps us to hear a range of sounds. The sound vibration reaches the eardrum and makes it vibrate. This in turn makes a series of small bones vibrate. Inside the inner ear, the vibrations of sound energy are converted to electrical energy which our nerves carry to the brain to translate into the words, music, or sounds that we hear.

What can we hear?

The lowest frequency that people can usually hear is around 20 Hz. This means that the lowest note you can hear vibrates 20 times in one second. The highest frequency humans hear is around 20 000 Hz. This can also be written as 20 kHz. The k stands for kilo and means thousands, like the k in km (1000 m).

Some people have difficulty hearing. This can be caused by a great variety of things. Such people can use hearing aids which amplify sounds, making them easier to hear. Some people who are profoundly deaf can sometimes be helped by medical treatment. This includes using a cochlea implant which sends signals artificially to the brain.

Sometimes, like the deaf percussionist, Evelyn Glennie, deaf people become very sensitive to the vibrations around them. Evelyn can sense the sounds she makes through her bare feet.

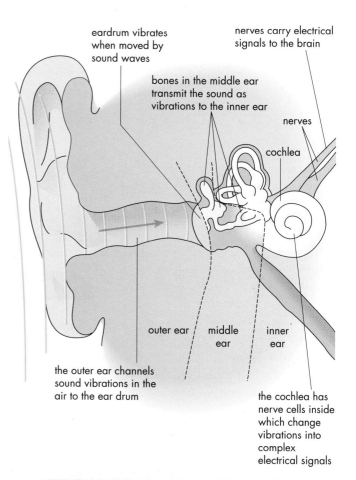

eardrum vibrates when moved by sound waves

nerves carry electrical signals to the brain

bones in the middle ear transmit the sound as vibrations to the inner ear

nerves

cochlea

outer ear

middle ear

inner ear

the outer ear channels sound vibrations in the air to the ear drum

the cochlea has nerve cells inside which change vibrations into complex electrical signals

Sound	Frequency (Hz)
middle C on piano	256
lowest note humans hear	20
highest note humans hear	20 000
small insect wings	1 000
bat sounds	130 000
elephant sounds	15

As we get older, our bodies change in many ways. Our hearing is at its best when we are about 10 years old. As we age, our hearing tends to get worse. The older we get the more we tend to loose the ability to hear high-pitched sounds. The chart shows how our hearing changes as we get older. Each line shows how well we hear at a particular age.

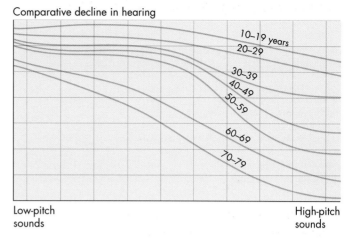

Comparative decline in hearing

10–19 years
20–29
30–39
40–49
50–59
60–69
70–79

Low-pitch sounds

High-pitch sounds

Hearing loss from age 10 to 80 years

ⓐ What is common to the hearing of all age groups?

ⓑ At what age does hearing for middle-pitch sounds get a lot worse?

ⓒ What age group of people might have difficulty hearing a mosquito? Explain your answer.

Are there sounds we can't hear?

There are sounds above our range of hearing (ultrasonics) and below our range of hearing (subsonics) that we can't hear.

Dogs can hear higher frequencies than we can, which is why they can hear a dog whistle and we can't. Bats use high-frequency sounds to find their way around in total darkness, even managing to find small, flying insects by bouncing sounds off them and listening to the echo. The bats can hear sounds with frequencies far higher than the ones we can hear. Elephants sometimes communicate with sounds of such a low frequency we cannot hear them.

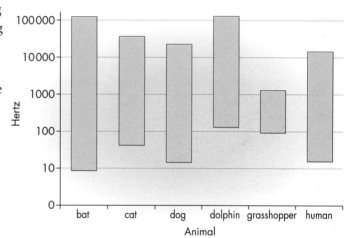

Hearing ranges of different animals

QUESTIONS

1 If you hold your lips and fingers against a balloon, you can feel the vibration of your voice on your fingertips. Explain how this works.

2 There are three bones in the middle ear. How do they help us to hear?

3 What do the hair cells in the cochlea do?

4 From the information on this page, which animal has the greatest range of hearing?

5 How is it that some people can hear low-frequency sounds but are deaf to higher-pitched sounds?

L4 CAN SOUND BE DANGEROUS?

TOPIC CHECKLIST

- Why are some sounds dangerous?
- What is noise pollution?
- How do we protect ourselves from noise?
- Which materials are the best sound insulators?

Why are some sounds dangerous?

If you are exposed to sounds which are too loud, your hearing can be permanently damaged. Loud music at night clubs or concerts can sometimes cause temporary deafness and may leave you with permanently poor hearing at some frequencies.

In our inner ear, there are nerve hairs cells which are moved by sound vibrations. These nerves generate tiny electric signals which are sent to the brain. If the sound vibrations are too intense, the nerve hair cells can be damaged. Then the nerve hair cells do not produce electrical signals and you do not hear the sound.

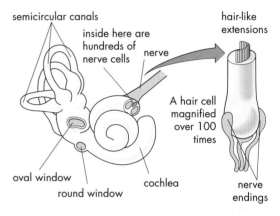

What is noise pollution?

Pollution is anything that has a bad effect on our environment. **Noise pollution** is loud, annoying, repetitive or spasmodic sounds. These can damage hearing, interfere with normal life or affect wildlife. Noise pollution is different from other forms of pollution – when the noise stops the pollutant disappears, although the effects can be permanent.

One of the most common sources of noise pollution is aircraft. The sound of large jet engines at take-off can be so loud that people living near a runway frequently have their lives disrupted.

Another type of noise pollution is loud noise at work. The loud sounds from drills used for road works are quite often damaging to the people using them. To help reduce the damage done to people's hearing at work, there are legal limits to the levels of noise in which people are allowed to work. Wearing ear protection is also a legal requirement for some types of job.

How do we protect ourselves from noise?

Reducing the volume of the sound made would seem to be the best idea, but this can be expensive or difficult to do. Another way to protect ourselves is to use a material that stops the vibrations passing through it. This is called an **insulating** material. It is usually soft and absorbs sound energy. The insulating material vibrates when the sound vibrations hit it and it transfers the sound energy into small amounts of heat energy. Ear defenders are made from insulating material. However, they have the drawback that you cannot hear other sounds around you.

Sound barriers are an excellent way of reducing the damage done by noise. Many roads with loud traffic noise have earth banks or walls between them and housing.

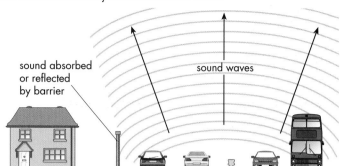

Another way of reducing sound is to reduce the reflection of the sound from the walls around you. When you go into a room with bare walls and floors, it is very noticeable that sounds echo loudly. If carpets are put down and curtains are hung, the sounds are absorbed by the soft materials and this stops the echoes.

Which materials are the best sound insulators?

Sound meters can be used to measure the level of sound. Peter and Jane decided to use a sound meter to investigate what the best sound insulator is. They set up a test chamber like the one shown in the picture. They placed a sound sensor at one end of one box, and the sound maker at the end of the other box. The boxes are placed on bubble wrap. The material to be tested is placed between the two boxes.

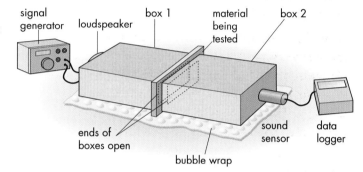

a Explain why the boxes are placed on bubble wrap.

b Why are two boxes used instead of one long one?

c Why is it important to keep the distance between the boxes constant?

Their results for a series of experiments are shown here. The values for sound level are on a scale of 1–100.

Material	Sound level
air (control)	87
cardboard	40
plywood	45
carpet	24
cotton wool	28
foam rubber	28

d Which of the materials was the best sound insulator?

e What do all the good sound insulators have in common?

f Why do you think plywood was the worst sound insulator apart from air?

QUESTIONS

1 Design an experiment to test the insulating effect of curtains on different frequencies of sound in a room.

2 The best sound insulators are soft materials with irregular surfaces rather than hard, flat surfaces. Explain why you think this is.

Why two ears?

Humans and many animals have two ears, but the position of the ears on the head varies in different animals. It has been suggested that two ears allow us to detect which direction a sound is coming from.

To test this you can blindfold someone and sit them in a quiet place. They face straight ahead while you make a sound from different directions but level with their ears and about one metre away. The person points to where they think the sound is coming from. The results from such an experiment are shown here. The circles show how good the person was in each direction.

ⓐ Describe any pattern you can see in the results.

ⓑ The chart shows results for the experiment using both ears and then the left and the right ears. Were two ears better than one?

ⓒ Were both ears as good as each other?

ⓓ Was this person more accurate in locating sounds in front, behind or to the sides?

Can ears affect hearing?

If we didn't have outer ears, we would still be able to hear but we might miss quiet sounds. The outer ear gathers sound and directs it towards the inner ear. Cupping a hand around the ear helps even more.

Below are two possible investigations into how ears affect what we hear.

1 To investigate how the size of the outer ears affects hearing.

2 To investigate how the position of the ears, pointing forwards or sideways, affects hearing.

To investigate either of these points you need to be quite clear about the question you are investigating.

Anatol decided to investigate an aspect of (1) asking 'Does the size of a person's ears affect their ability to hear quiet sounds?'.

He suggests an hypothesis, based on his science knowledge. 'People with larger outer ears can hear quieter sounds because more sound energy is directed into the auditory canal'.

The variable he measured was the area of a person's ear. He used human subjects with different ear sizes. To measure the area of the outer ear, he multiplied the ear height by the ear width.

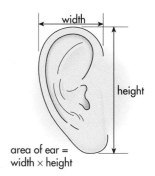

area of ear = width × height

The variables he decided to keep the same were: age of subjects, time of day, what sounds they have been exposed to recently, distance from sound, direction of sound, frequency of sound, surroundings.

He carried out the experiment and recorded the results and looked to see whether there was a link between ear size and hearing. He plotted a scatter graph of the results.

He decided that the results supplied strong evidence for the hypothesis. His teacher told him if the results hadn't given strong evidence then he might have needed to do some more investigations.

Finally, he compared his results with those of other pupils in the class. To make sure Anatol's experimental results were accurate, he asked his friend to perform a similar experiment to see if he got the same results. One of the key pieces of evidence scientists use to work out how convincing another scientist's results are, is whether the results can be reproduced in other laboratories.

How good are ear defenders?

Another investigation you might try is to find out how good ear defenders are. To do this you can move a sound source away from a person until they cannot hear it anymore. Then try the experiment again with different makes of ear defenders, or ear defenders made by a number of groups in your class. The best ear defenders will be the ones where the sound is closest but cannot be heard.

e **Decide what you will investigate, what factors you will keep the same and write a plan for your investigation.**

Solving noise pollution

Below is a case study on noise pollution. You are a consultant called in to look at the situation.

'When an industrial unit was rented by a metal products fabrication company, local residents complained to the district council about the high-pitched irritating noise made by the metal-grinding machines.'

f **Suggest three different methods that the company could use to reduce the sound levels reaching the residents. Explain how each of your ideas would work.**

Glossary

absorb (biology)   when living cells or blood take in food or oxygen

absorbs (physics)   light **energy** hits a surface and is converted into heat **energy**

accumulate   to build up

accumulation   the process of building up or gathering together

acidic   has a pH less than 7, for example stomach acid

adaptations   features of organisms which help them to survive or to do their job

aerobic respiration   glucose from food reacts with oxygen to release **energy**

alkaline   has a pH greater than 7

alveoli   air sacs in the lungs where **gaseous exchange** happens

amplitude   the size of a wave

amylase enzyme   **enzyme** responsible for the breakdown of starch

anaerobic respiration   chemical reactions that release **energy** without oxygen

angle of incidence   angle between the normal and an incident ray

angle of reflection   angle between the normal and a reflected ray

angle of refraction   angle between the normal and a refracted ray

antibodies   chemicals produced by certain **white blood cells**, which help to destroy **microbes**

anus   the end point of the **digestive system**

apparent depth   when objects in water appear closer to the surface than they are

arteries   blood vessels that carry blood away from the heart

atoms   the smallest bit of something

attraction   force pulling towards something

balanced diet   range of **nutrients** needed to stay healthy

bar magnet   rectangular type of magnet with poles at each end

bed   layer of rock; a stratum

bedding plane   the boundary between one **bed** and the next

bimetallic strip   device which moves as **temperature** changes, often part of an electronic heating control system

bleach   remove the colour from a substance

blood   fluid responsible for transporting substances from one part of the body to another

body temperature   maintained **temperature** of body, in humans 37 °C

boiling point   the **temperature** at which a pure substance changes from a liquid to a gas (or a gas to a liquid)

burial   when **sediments** are covered over by new sediments or other material

capillaries   small blood vessels with thin walls, which carry blood between the arteries and veins

carbohydrate   group of **energy**-rich substances, for example starch and sugar

carnivore   an animal that eats only other animals

cement   the material that 'glues' rock **grains** together

cementation   the process of 'gluing' rock **grains** together

cemented   stuck, or glued, together

change of state	material changing state between solid, liquid or gas	**convection current**	flow of liquids or gases due to **convection**
characteristics	distinctive features	**cornea**	outer **transparent** surface of the eye
chemical (properties)	**properties** concerning changes that involve the formation of a new substance	**cystic fibrosis**	inherited disease which affects breathing
chemical change	a change that involves the formation of a new substance	**decay**	rotting process involving bacteria and fungi where **nutrients** are released from **detritus**
chemical digestion	**digestion** of food which involves chemicals called **enzymes**	**decibels**	unit of sound measurement
chemical formula	shorthand of symbols and numbers used to represent a chemical compound	**degrees Celsius**	common unit for **temperature** measurement
		deposition	when **sediments** are put down or dropped
chemical reaction	the process of change from **reactants** to **products**	**detritus**	waste and dead material
chlorine	a green non-metallic **element** that is a poisonous gas	**digestion**	the process by which food is broken down into smaller particles
community	all the different **species** living in a **habitat**	**digestive system**	the organs involved in **digestion**
compacted	squashed by forces underground that are caused by rock movements	**dispersion**	splitting light into a **spectrum**
		double pump	the right-hand side of the heart pumps blood to the lungs; the left-hand side pumps blood to the rest of the body
compaction	the process of squashing rocks		
compound	a pure substance made of two or more kinds of **atom** that are chemically joined		
		Earth's magnetic field	**magnetic field** around the Earth
condenses	changes from gas to liquid state	**echo**	sound reflected off a surface
conduction	movement of **energy** through a solid	**ecosystem**	the **habitat** and the **community** interacting within it
conductor	material that is good at letting heat **energy** pass through it	**egested**	when undigested waste leaves the body via the **anus**
consumers	animals which must eat other living things for food	**electromagnet**	magnet formed by electric current passing through a coil around a wire
contracts	material getting shorter and thinner as it cools	**elements**	the simplest substances
convection	liquids or gases moving due to differences in **temperature** and density	**energy**	ability to do work
		energy transfer	**energy** changing from one form to another

environmental conditions	the conditions in a **habitat** which affect what can survive there	**grains**	the usually small fragments or crystals that make up a rock
enzymes	chemicals found in the **digestive system**, used to break down large particles into smaller ones	**grow**	increase in size
		habitat	the place where an animal or plant lives
erosion	the combination of **weathering** and **transport**	**herbivore**	an animal that eats only plants
evaporation	change of state from liquid to gas at the surface of the liquid	**igneous rocks**	rocks formed from molten (melted) material
exfoliates	breaks off in layers	**immunity**	**antibodies** already in your blood recognise **microbes** and stop them causing disease
exhale	breathe out air from the lungs		
expands	material gets longer and thicker as it gets warmer	**impurities**	unwanted parts of a mixture
		incident ray	light ray that hits a surface
expire	breathe out air from the lungs	**infection**	having a **microbe** present in your body, usually causes symptoms
faeces	undigested waste product which leaves the body via the **anus**	**infectious**	being able to pass on a disease
fat	substance found in food, used as an **energy** store and part of cell membranes	**infra-red radiation**	heat **energy** moving like visible light
		inhale	breathe air into the lungs
fermentation	breakdown of a substance by bacteria or yeasts, usually without oxygen	**inspire**	breathe air into the lungs
		insulator, insulating	material that reduces the amount of heat, electricity or sound **energy** moving through it
fibre	indigestible food which keeps your **digestive system** working properly		
filtered	solid bits are separated from a mixture	**interlocking**	rock **grains** that fit together without any gaps between them
food chain	a diagram showing what an animal eats and what eats it	**iris**	coloured ring that controls the size of the **pupil** in a human eye
food web	a diagram made of lots of joined up **food chains**, showing what eats what in a **habitat** and the flow of **energy** in that habitat	**lactic acid**	by-product of **anaerobic respiration**, causes aching muscles
		lateral inversion	objects appear back to front when seen reflected in a mirror
fossils	remains of plant or animal material found in rock	**lava**	molten rock on the surface of the Earth
freezes	changes from liquid to solid state	**lens**	part of the eye that focuses light onto the **retina**
frequency	how often something happens		
gaseous exchange	when oxygen passes into the blood and carbon dioxide moves out of the blood; takes place in the **alveoli** in the lungs	**light year**	distance light travels in one year
		luminous	object that gives off light
		magma	molten rock underground
geologist	a scientist who studies the Earth		

magnetic field	region where there is a magnetic force	**odourless**	having no smell
magnetic field lines	lines showing which way a magnetic **north pole** would move	**omnivore**	an animal that eats both plants and animals
mechanical digestion	**digestion** of food which involves physical action to break food into smaller pieces, for example chewing	**opaque**	a material that does not allow visible light to pass through it
medium	material that **energy**, e.g. sound or heat, passes through	**oxygen**	a colourless, non-metallic **element** that is a gas involved in burning
melting point	the **temperature** at which a pure substance changes from a solid to a liquid (or a liquid to a solid)	**pathogen**	organism which causes disease
		penicillin	first antibiotic discovered by Sir Alexander Fleming
metamorphic rocks	rocks formed from other rocks changed by heat and pressure	**Periodic Table**	the table showing all the **elements**
microbes	tiny organisms which can only be seen using a microscope	**physical (properties)**	**properties** concerning changes that do not involve the formation of a new substance
minerals	substances required in small amounts by the body/chemical compounds found in rocks	**pitch**	how high or low a sound is
mnemonic	an easily remembered phrase to remind you of the initial letters of a list (e.g. MRS. GREN)	**plant kingdom**	group of living things which make their food using chlorophyll and light energy
Mohs' scale	scale used to compare the hardness of **minerals**	**plasma**	fluid part of the blood which carries everything apart from oxygen around the body
molecule	a group of **atoms** that are chemically joined together	**population size**	number of individuals in a **species** in a specific area at a specific time
mouth	beginning of the **digestive system** where food enters the body	**porous**	a rock with spaces between the **grains**
noise pollution	sound which is a nuisance	**predator**	an animal which hunts other animals for food
non-interlocking	rock grains that fit together with gaps between them	**prescription**	form written by a doctor to get medicines, includes antibiotics
non-luminous	object that does not give off light	**prey**	an animal which is hunted and eaten by another animal
normal	line at right angles to a surface	**primary colours**	three colours seen by the human eye
north pole	end of magnet which repels a north pole	**primary consumer**	the first animal in a **food chain**; it always eats the **producer**
nutrients	substances in your food which are needed and used by your body	**producers**	plants which produce their own food using energy from the Sun
nutritional label	label found on food packaging which states the amount of each **nutrient** in a particular food	**product**	a substance that is made during a **chemical change**
		properties	the **characteristics** of a substance

protein	food needed for growth and repair of tissues, also used to make **enzymes**	**scurvy**	disease caused by a lack of **vitamin C** in the diet
pupil	the hole in the eye that allows light in	**secondary consumer**	the second animal in a **food chain**; it always eats the **primary consumer**
pyramid of numbers	a diagram showing the number of **organisms** at each level of a **food chain**	**sedimentary rocks**	rocks formed from deposited rock fragments
ray diagram	diagram that shows which way light rays travel	**sediments**	fragments of broken rock
reactants	substances that react together during a **chemical change**	**sexually transmitted disease**	microbes passed onto others during sexual intercourse
recommended daily allowance (RDA)	suggested amount of each nutrient which is needed daily to stay healthy	**shadow**	area of darkness where light is blocked by an object
red blood cells	cells in the blood which carry oxygen around the body	**sickle-cell anaemia**	inherited disease which affects the blood's ability to carry oxygen
reflected ray	light ray that bounces off a surface	**skin**	main barrier our bodies have against microbe **infection**
reflects	light bounces off a surface	**sodium**	a silvery metallic **element** that explodes on contact with water
refraction	bending of light when it moves from one material to another	**source**	place which light or heat comes from
repulsion	force pushing something away	**south pole**	end of magnet which attracts a **north pole**
resistant	when bacteria are not affected by antibiotics	**species**	living things which have almost all of their features in common
retina	light-sensitive surface at the back of the eye	**spectrum**	a range of light colours
rickets	disease caused by a lack of **vitamin D** in the diet	**state of matter**	the three states of matter are solid, liquid and gas
rock cycle	a way (usually a diagram) of linking all the processes involved in the formation of rocks	**subscript**	a number or letter that is written slightly below the normal line of the text
roots	part of the plant usually below ground which anchor the plant and absorb **nutrients**	**sulphur**	a solid, yellow, non-metallic **element**
rot	substances broken down by chemical action of **microbes**	**symbol**	sign that means something
sample	the measured area used for **sampling**	**temperature**	how hot or cold a material is
sampling	method for estimating the **population size**	**texture**	the way that rock **grains** fit together
scattered	disorganisation of light	**thermal energy**	heat **energy** in a material
		thermometer	device for measuring **temperature**
		translucent	a material that scatters visible light as the light passes through it

transmission	light passing through a material/a method for passing microbes onto another person
transparent	a material that allows visible light to pass through it without scattering
transport	the process of moving rock fragments from one place to another
uplifting	the process of rocks being moved from deep underground to the surface of the Earth
vaccine	substance put into your blood to make you **immune** to certain **microbes**
vacuum	space with no material in it
veins	blood vessels that carry blood towards the heart
vibrate	to move back and forward rapidly
viscous	thick, sticky liquid
vitamins	substances required in small amounts by the body
weathering	the process of changing a rock by natural processes
white blood cells	cells in the blood which defend the body against infection
word equation	a way of recording a **chemical change**

Index

retina 129
rickets 36
rock cycle 98–99
rocks 76–77
    density 96–97
    textures 77
    transport of 82–83
    weathering of 78–81
roots, nutrients absorbed through 53
rotting 28, 53

salt 65
    effect on boiling/melting points
        of water/ice 74–75
sampling 48
sand 76
sandstone 76, 77, 89
    metamorphic rock from 93
scattering of light 126
schist 93
scurvy 4, 37
secondary consumers (in food web)
    50
sedimentary rocks 88–89, 98, 99
sediments 83
    compaction of 86–87, 88
    deposition of 84–85, 88
seeing things 128–129
sexually transmitted diseases 33
shadows 124
shale 89
    metamorphic rock from 93
sickle-cell anaemia 37
skin, as barrier 36
slate 76, 92, 93
small intestine
    digestion in 10, 13
    model 11, 13
Snow, Dr John 34
sodium chloride 64, 65
solidifying of liquids 74
sound
    speed in air 139
    travelling through gas/liquid/solid
        138–139
    ways of reducing 142–143
sound meters 137, 143
sounds
    hearing 140–141
    making 136
south magnetic pole 116, 120

special diets 7
spectrum 133
starch, breakdown of 11, 12–13
states of matter 114
    changing 114–115
stirring rod thermometer 101
stomach, digestion in 10, 13
subscript in chemical formula 66, 67
sulphide 64, 65
sulphur 57, 65
sulphur dioxide 69
Sun
    heat energy from 112
    light from 124
symbols for elements 55, 56–57, 67

temperature 100–101
    effect on rocks 80–81
    and heat energy 104–105
textures 77
thermal contraction 108
thermal energy 102
thermal expansion 108–109
thermometers 100, 101
thunder and lightning 139
translucent materials 126
transmission of diseases 33
transmission of light 126, 127
transparent materials 126
transport of rocks 82–83
travertine 90
tuberculosis 40–41
tufa (rock) 91
tuning fork 136

uplifting of rocks 94

vaccination 42–43
vacuum 112, 124, 138
veins 22
ventricles (of heart) 22
Vesalius, Andreas 24
vibrating objects 136
viruses 29
    diseases caused by 32, 35, 39
viscous liquid, magma as 94
Visking tubing 12, 13
vitamins
    effects of deficiencies 4, 37
    sources 3
    use by body 4

wartime rationing 6
water
    arrangement of atoms in 57, 60,
        61, 66
    boiling point 74, 75, 100, 114, 115
    changes of state 114
    chemical formula for 67, 69
    freezing point 74, 100, 114, 115
    importance in body 5, 15
    output from body 15, 20
    production by plants 27
    properties compared with
        elements 68
    sound waves in 138
    sources 3
weathering of rocks 78–81
white blood cells 20, 36, 42
word equations 63

yeast 30
yellow fever 35
yoghurt 30